WORKING TO RULE

Railway Workshop Rules: a study of industrial discipline by

KENNETH HUDSON

ADAMS & DART

© 1970 Kenneth Hudson

First published in 1970 by Adams & Dart, 40 Gay Street, Bath
SBN 239.00057.9
Printed and bound in Great Britain by
C. Tinling & Company Limited, Prescot

Contents

Acknowledgements

I should like to thank the many people who have provided me with material and suggested new sources of information. The staff of British Rail's Historical Records Department, both at York and Porchester Road, gave me a great deal of help. So did the Branch Secretaries of the National Union of Railwaymen in Crewe, Derby, Darlington and Swindon, and a number of present-day members of the staff at Wolverton, Crewe, Swindon and Derby Works. Among the many railway veterans who have given me the benefit of their long memories, I should like to express my particular gratitude to Mr R. A. Riddles, Mr F. B. Townsend, Mr A. Healey, Mr Wilfred Charlesworth, Mr Harry Pearce, Mr J. O. Hughes, Mr W. Lawrence and Mr Leslie Cooper.

I have been treated with great kindness by the staff of the University Library at Bristol, by the County Archivists of Durham and Buckinghamshire, and by the Borough Librarians at Swindon, Crewe and Derby. Mr Robert J. Ayers, of the Wolverton and District Archaeological Society, has discovered a number of useful items of which I should otherwise have been ignorant, and Mr Harold Plaister has put his unequalled knowledge of Swindon personalities at my disposal.

A special word of thanks is due to Mr C. Tilling, of Dunstable, who first drew my attention to the Rule Books of the Railway Works, and thereby started me on a line of inquiry which has brought me many hours of pleasure.

1

THE PERISHABILITY
OF RULE BOOKS

ARMIES and navies have always been governed by strict rules; apprentices, from medieval times onward, have been compelled to sign indentures which provided for a tight control over their working behaviour; domestic servants in large establishments had to fit into a precise hierarchy and follow a clearly laid-down pattern of instructions.

Sailors, domestic servants and factory workers are merely different kinds of employee, prone to idle, to avoid unpleasant tasks, to steal, to drink and to be dirty and untidy in their habits whenever the eye of the master is not fixed steadily and menacingly on them. This sad truth is as well known to Marks & Spencers and the manager of the Savoy as it was to Admiral Boscawen and the mistress of a large Victorian household. All employers, in consequence, attempt to discipline and control the labour they engage. Some achieve this better than others, according to their skill and temperament and to the sanctions they are able to apply. Slaves and soldiers operate under the constant threat of severe penalties, including death, if they disobey orders. Present-day car-workers, on the other hand, are almost impossible to discipline, because they are not worried about losing their jobs and because they are in a position to cause a great deal of trouble if their wishes are not met.

If the working unit is small—a fishing boat, a shoe-shop, or a farm—it is unlikely that the rules and regulations which are to be followed will be written down in any great detail. The person in charge will tell the new recruit what he is supposed to do. During the eighteenth and nineteenth centuries, however, two new tendencies made this man-to-man, informal type of discipline steadily less possible. One was the growth of large manufacturing units and the other was the necessity for the State to prevent workers from being grossly exploited by powerful and impersonal employers.

The men who built up and ran the big industrial enterprises which characterised the Industrial Revolution and gave it shape and direction were, as Professor Peter Matthias has pointed out,[1] distinguished as organisers, not as pioneers of major innovations or inventions. They had to control the conditions of production to a degree never previously envisaged or attempted and they were ruthless in the methods they used in order to do this.

The sheer control of a large labour force was perhaps their major difficulty in the eighteenth century. There was a self-imposed family discipline in cottage industry, the hours of work and intensity of work decided by the master of the family. Men commonly worked furiously at the end of the week to finish the piece of cloth or their stint in nailing by Saturday when the merchant collected it. They were then idle or drunk until the following Tuesday, having kept "Saint Monday". By contrast, in the factory regularity was the prerequisite. All the machines were geared to the engine, and the entire sequence of production demanded that each worker subordinate his own will to that of the whole working unit. The extraordinary codes of discipline, with fines and sanctions, imposed by large-scale industrialists like Ambrose Crowley, Richard Arkwright and Wedgwood are understandable in the light of the great problems of imposing standards of discipline and regularity on an untrained labour force.[2]

Professor Sidney Pollard has made a detailed study[3] of the methods used by eighteenth-century factory-owners to enforce discipline on workers who showed small understanding of what the machine was beginning to do to their working lives. 'The very recruitment to the uncongenial work was difficult,' he reminds us, 'and it was made worse by the deliberate or accidental modelling of many works on workhouses and prisons, a fact well known to the working population'.[4] The new industrial proletariat was much given to staying away from work, to poor timekeeping, to taking breaks during the day and, above all, to wandering from job to job: 'It was not necessarily the better labourer, but the stable one who was worth the most to the manufacturer', Professor Pollard emphasises.

Faced with a labour force which they were bound to regard as feckless, idle and immoral, the new-style eighteenth-century employers devoted much energy and ingenuity to drawing up and enforcing detailed codes of behaviour. The best known codes were those of Josiah Wedgwood (1780), the Soho Foundry (1796), Heathcote's at Tiverton, the Wear Cotton Mills, Alexander Galloway and John Marshall. 'So strict are the instructions,' it was said of John Marshall's flax mills in 1821, 'that if an overseer of a room be found talking to any person in the mill during working hours he is dismissed immediately. Two or more overseers are employed in each room. If one be found a yard out of his ground, he is discharged. Everyone, manager, overseers, mechanics, oilers, spreaders, spinners and reelers, have their particular duty pointed out to them, and if they transgress they are instantly turned off as unfit for their situation.'[5]

The main deterrents to misbehaviour were dismissal and the threat of dismissal.

At times of labour shortage they were ineffective, but when a buyer's market in labour returned, a sigh of relief went through the ranks of the employers at the restoration of their power. Many abolished the apprenticeship system in order to gain it, and without it others were unable to keep any control whatsoever. Where there were no competing mill employers, as at Shrewsbury in the case of Marshall and Benyon's flax mills, it was a most effective threat.[6]

Men with exceptional skill and experience were unlikely to be dismissed, even in times when business was bad. The employer who gave summary treatment to people who were likely to be very difficult to replace was not likely to prosper. It was, however, always possible to fine a man as an alternative to dismissing him and by the end of the eighteenth century this had become standard practice, both in industries employing skilled men and in those employing mostly women and children.

The level of fines was high in relation to the current rate of wages. A fine, as Professor Pollard has pointed out,

was meant to hurt. Typically they were levied at 6d. to 2s. for ordinary offences, or, say, two hours to a day's wages. Wedgwood fined 2s. 6d. for throwing things or for leaving fires burning overnight, and that was also the penalty for being absent on Monday mornings in the Worsley mines. At Fernley's Stockport mill swearing, singing or being drunk were punished by a fine of 5s. and so was stealing coal at Mertbys. Miners were fined even more heavily: average weekly deductions were alleged to be as high as 1s. or 2s. out of a wage of 13s.[7]

The later eighteenth century had a number of enterprises with several hundred workers. These included the Royal dockyards and arsenals, a few textile mills, and one or two ironworks and engineering factories, of which Boulton and Watt's Soho Works was the largest. Concerns of this size could not be run without detailed regulations. Such regulations were relatively easy to enforce because unemployment, hunger and homelessness were ever-present realities. Working men and women needed their jobs and they were prepared to put up with a great deal in order to keep them.

This situation continued throughout the nineteenth century and, indeed, up to the outbreak of war in 1939. It is not easy for anyone who entered the labour market after that date to understand why their fathers and grandfathers tolerated such long working hours, such a low standard of amenities and such depressed wages. Consequently, both the provisions of the early Factory Acts and the rules drawn up and enforced by individual employers are likely to seem somewhat unreal and much farther away in time than they really are.

The railways, from the beginning, were employers on an unprecedented scale. Tens of thousands of men were needed to build them and tens of thousands to run them and to make and repair their equipment. The prospects of regular employment and promotion were exceptionally good in an industry whose labour force expanded from 47,000 in 1847 to 127,000 in 1860 and 274,000 in 1873. Until recently, no serious research has been carried out to discover where, in fact, the railways found the men they needed during the 1830's and 1840's. Mr G. L. Turnbull now suggests[8] that for general staffing a good deal of the labour required was absorbed from the coaching trade, which had been rapidly put out of business by the coming of the railways. The men mainly involved had been the drivers and guards of the express coaches—the local, short-distance coaches survived longer—book-keepers, and ostlers.

For management staff the railways went to some extent to ex-army officers, but much more, in Mr Turnbull's opinion, to the carrying trade and, in particular, to Pickfords, where there was a considerable reservoir of 'skilled and experienced men who were capable of supervising the complex and detailed operations of a railway'.

Many of the men required for the humbler posts were recruited from agriculture. It is not difficult to see why. Although railway porters averaged only 18s. 7d. a week in 1850 and worked at least twelve hours a day, they were substantially better off than the farm labourer whose wages averaged 11s. 6d. a week in the North of England and only 8s. 5d. in the South. But it was not only the rural population that found its way into railway jobs. Mr B. J. Turton has looked carefully[9] at the 1851 Census returns for three Southern towns with large railway workshops—Swindon, Ashford and Wolverton—and remarks on 'the substantial proportion of residents drawn from the industrial counties of Lancashire, Yorkshire, Durham and Northumberland, which were the counties containing the leading engineering districts at this date'.

Skilled men and reliable, trainable men in the unskilled grades were difficult to find in the 1830's and 1840's. The railway companies found themselves faced with a considerable problem. On the one hand, they were anxious to attract and hold good workers, and on the other they felt obliged to enforce an extremely high standard of discipline. If railway employees were careless in their work, the result was all too likely to be a disaster involving death or injury to passengers, of whom 30 million were carried in 1845, 67 million in 1850 and 111 million in 1855. So this first generation of drivers, porters, signalmen and guards was told exactly what to do, strictly supervised and dismissed or fined in the event of any failure of duty. They had no tradition to absorb, no family know-how to help them along, no experience of working in large organisations. Learning had to be a rapid process and it was encouraged by fear of punishment. During the year ending 31 July 1841, the Great Western dismissed 79 out of its total labour force of 700.

Parliament gave its full support to the directors' policy that the safe working of railway traffic required the maintenance of a strict labour discipline. The Select Committee on Railways gave its opinion, in 1839, that it was 'essential to the safety of the public and to the maintenance of regular intercourse by railroads, that companies should have more perfect control over their servants'. This 'more perfect control' was achieved by regulations adopted in 1840 and 1842 which provided that a railway servant who broke the rules in any way could be brought before the magistrate immediately and given either a two months' prison sentence or a fine of £10. Only the highest standard of conduct could be tolerated. During the first three decades of railway history, porters were fined if they were caught accepting tips from passengers.

It is only fair to point out, however, that the companies did not rely entirely on prison, fines and dismissal as a way of building up a satisfactory staff. They went to great pains to encourage loyalty in more positive ways, by providing cheap coal, free clothing, company housing and end-of-year bonuses. Sureties were demanded from those occupying positions where exceptional trustworthiness was required and the then widespread habit of one of the directors of a railway company personally nominating a man to a post was thought, probably correctly, to engender useful feelings of gratitude to the company. But the basis of good conduct was a painstakingly drawn-up and meticulously enforced set of rules and regulations.

On the operating side, the railway rule book has become a national institution. 'Working to rule' is a railwayman's phrase that has passed into the language. The regulations that drivers and guards and signalmen are supposed to follow are so numerous and so precise that to observe them to the letter is to bring the railways almost to a standstill. Few workers anywhere have been so exactly and comprehensively instructed as the British railwayman.

Considerable numbers of these operating rule books survive, including many from the nineteenth century. There are, however, connoisseurs' items to be discovered within this field, outside the rule books themselves. One delightful set of very specialised rules, dated 1899, is preserved in the archives at Wolverton Works. It consists of seventeen instructions to 'Guards and Attendants in charge of corridor trains, corridor vehicles, dining saloons or sleeping cars' on the London and North Western and Caledonian Railways.

1. The Guards must make the safe and punctual working of the Train their first care, and nothing must be allowed to interfere with their duty in this respect.
2. The rear Guard must only leave his van while the Train is travelling in the case of absolute necessity.
3. The Train Attendants must make themselves thoroughly acquainted with the Rules in the Rule Book relating to Guards' duties, and with the Vacuum and Westinghouse Break Instructions, and also those relating to the Steam Heating Apparatus, and be prepared to act as Assistant Guards in cases of emergency. The men must be examined periodically by the District Officers.
4. The Guards and Train Attendants must be on duty 30 minutes before starting time, and assist in the seating of Passengers generally, placing those who do not require Luncheon or Dinner in the ordinary compartments.
5. The Guards and Train Attendants must report an any case where the marshalling of their Train does not obviate, as far as possible, Third Class Passengers having to pass through the First Class Dining Cars and Corridors to reach the Third Class Dining Cars.
6. All Break Van Doors leading to the Corridors, and all dividing doors between the First Class and Third Class Corridors, must be kept locked throughout the entire journey, excepting when Passengers are being personally conducted to and from the Dining Saloons by the Attendants; and it must be thoroughly understood by the men in charge of the Train that the object of the Corridor system is not to give Passengers the opportunity of promenading the whole length of the Train, but to afford means of access to and from the Dining, Luncheon, or Breakfast Saloons, and give each Passenger the use of a Lavatory.
7. The Lavatory Doors must be kept closed, and the Lavatories themselves frequently inspected en route. The Carriage Department on the London and North Western Line and the Superintendent's Department on the Caledonian Line will be responsible for supplying each Lavatory with towels and soap at the starting point, but this will not relieve the men in charge of the Train of the responsibility of keeping the Lavatories in proper order throughout the journey.
8. The Dining Car Attendants (assisted by the Train Attendants when such are on the Train) must ascertain what Passengers require Luncheon, and when that meal is ready they must conduct the Passengers to the Cars, locking the dividing doors after this

has been done. After Luncheon the Dining Car Attendants must conduct the Passengers back to their compartments, unlocking and relocking the doors, as laid down in paragraph 6. The same plan must be adopted at other meals.

9. When the Electric Bell rings the Train Attendant (if there is one on the Train) must promptly attend to the requirements of the Passenger, and the Guards and Dining Car Attendants must in such cases lose no time in taking steps to acquaint the Train Attendant with the fact that the Passengers' Bell is ringing (in the case of Trains fitted throughout with improved Bell communication, a code between Van and Van will be laid down for the purpose of making clear in what portion of the Train the Passengers' Bell is ringing).

10. The Dining and Sleeping Saloon Attendants will be held responsible for seeing that their Cars are supplied with the current issue of the Time Tables, and in the case of the Corridor Dining Trains, the Train Attendant must keep himself supplied with the Special Note Paper, &c., for the use of Passengers.

11. Letter Boxes provided in the Saloons of the Corridor Trains must be cleared by the Train Attendant, in accordance with the instructions painted on the Boxes. Where there is no Train Attendant, the man in charge of the Saloon in which the Box is placed will be held responsible for this duty.

12. The Dining Saloon Attendants will be held responsible for seeing that portmanteaus and heavy bags, or other bulky luggage, are not brought into their Cars to block up the corridors and lobbies; where there is a Train Attendant he is responsible for the same duty, so far as it relates to ordinary Corridor Carriages; where there is no Attendant provided, the Guard must see that the Corridors are kept free; and all Servants in charge of Corridor Vehicles must thoroughly understand that the Corridors are to be kept perfectly clear of Luggage, everything too large to be placed in compartment racks being taken into the Van. Dogs are not to be allowed in the Corridors, neither is smoking to be permitted here.

13. When Vehicles have to be detached on the journey, it will be the special duty of the men in charge to see that the Corridor Door on each side of the gangway at the point of separation is locked before the operation of detaching is commenced. The responsibility for this will devolve as follows : —
   (a) In the case of Sleeping Saloon Vehicles, or of other Vehicles connected thereto by gangway, on the Sleeping Saloon Attendant.
   (b) In the case of Dining Carriages and all other Vehicles, on the Train Attendant, if there is one; otherwise upon the Guard of the portion of the Train affected.

14. The Train Attendants, and all other Servants, must exercise vigilance during the journey, with a view to preventing Passengers taking First Class Seats with Third Class Tickets after the Ticket Examiners have been through the Train.

15. The windows in the Corridors and Compartments must be kept closed when Passengers do not require them to be open.
16. The Train Attendants must exercise careful supervision over the Gas consumed in the Roof Lamps and Heating Apparatus, and see that the greatest economy, compatible with efficiency, is exercised in its use.
17. The Train Attendants must, on the termination of each journey, send in promptly to Mr. Turnbull at Euston, and to Mr. Kempt at Glasgow, a report on the printed form provided for the purpose, mentioning any difficulty which may have arisen, and offering any suggestion which may occur to them for meeting such difficulty. They must also mention in their reports all cases where the accommodation in the Train is insufficient for the traffic, and Passengers holding different classes of Tickets have to be mixed.

It would be an exaggeration to say that, in one way and another the discipline involved in running trains is fully and continuously documented from the earliest days. Yet the material is ample, whereas the rule books and rule-sheets for the railway workshops are exceedingly rare and I have had to search very hard indeed for the examples reproduced in this book[10]. 'I am very sorry,' wrote the Curator of Historical Relics to the British Railway Board, 'that we have no information of the sort you are seeking. So far as I know, works rules and regulations are very scarce, having largely perished.' 'Unfortunately,' replied the General Secretary of the National Union of Vehicle Builders, 'we have no rule books in our possession such as you require.' I have had to learn to get used to letters like this; they came in an almost unbroken sequence. From the General Secretary of the National Union of Railwaymen: 'Whilst I would be very pleased to assist I am afraid there is nothing here that would help you in your enquiries. You will appreciate, of course, that in the distant days to which you refer there were individual and private Railway Companies and, whilst it is possible that at one time copies of the various documents were available through contact with individual members working in the shops, these have gradually disappeared throughout the passing years.'

THE earliest set of regulations I have come across relates to the Works of the Stockton and Darlington Railway at New Shildon. It is dated 17 August 1833, and is in poster form. It hangs in the Students' Room at the Railway Archives in York.

RULES AND REGULATIONS
to be observed by
The Workmen
in the employ of the
Stockton and Darlington Railway Company
at
NEW SHILDON

I   The Meal Times allowed, are from 8 to half past 8 o'Clock in the Morning, for Breakfast; and from 12 to 1, for Dinner, at all times of the year.

II   Overtime to be reckoned at the rate of 8 hours for a Day; but no Overtime to be entered till a whole Day of regular time has been worked.

III Every Workman to put on his Time-board with his Time, the name of the article or articles he has been working at during the Day, and what Engine or other Machinery they are for.

IV   Every Workman who is provided with a Drawer, for his Tools, with Lock and Key, the Drawer and his Key to be numbered, and all his Tools to be marked with the same Number, and the letters SDRWC; the key to be left at the Office every night when the man has left work.

V   Any Workman who is longer than a quarter of an hour after the Bell is rung, will lose a Quarter Day.

VI   Any Workman who does not call for his Time-Board in the

Morning, and return it to the Office in the Evening, or when done
work, to be fined SIXPENCE.

VII   Any Workman leaving his work without giving notice to the
Clerk or to the Foreman, to be fined ONE SHILLING.

VIII   Any Workman swearing, or using abusive language to a shop-
mate, to be fined ONE SHILLING.

IX   Should any one or more send for Beer, Ale or Spirits, into the
Works (without leave), to be fined ONE SHILLING.

X   Any Workman introducing a Stranger, or any person into the
Works (without leave), to be fined ONE SHILLING.

XI   Any Workman giving in more time than he has wrought, to have
double the time taken off that he has overcharged.

XII   The Company's Time-Piece at the Shops, to be the guide to the
Workmen's time.

XIII   Any Workman taking Tools from a Lathe or other piece of
Machinery, to be fined SIXPENCE.

XIV   Any Workman not returning Taps or Dies, or any general Tool,
to the person, who has the charge of them, to be fined
SIXPENCE.

XV   Should any Workman leave his work for the purpose of Drinking,
in working hours, he will be considered as having forfeited his
situation.

It appears, however, that the Stockton and Darlington applied at least
part of the proceeds of its fining system to welfare purposes. A Committee Minute of 12 January 1838, reads: 'Agreed: To allow Edward
Bell 20s. out of the fine box toward the expenses of a new wooden leg.'

An employee of the Stockton and Darlington Railway broke the Com-
pany's rules at his peril. There were plenty of other men who were
anxious to step into his job, as the Chairman of the Board, the Quaker
Edward Pease, made clear in his evidence to the Select Committee on
Railways in 1839.[1] He appeared, together with his colleague, Samuel
Barnard. The dialogue went like this:

'Does it occur to you, the companies at present have sufficient authority over their servants ?—*We find no difficulty in that respect; we fine a
man twice, the third time we discharge him.*

You find your authority quite abundant? *I think every week, in consequence of the great number we have employed (nearly 100 men and
assistants), we have brought up for default, the smallest penalty is 2s. 6d.,
sometimes we fine them as high as £1.*

There is no difficulty in replacing them? *We keep a large number of
young men as supernumeraries.*

Do you retain their wages, or have you some specific agreement with
each servant? *There is no specific agreement, the bye-laws are hung up, and
it is the business of the engineman when a new one is made, or the inspector of*

the engine power, to make the men individually acquainted with the new bye-law, which is posted in a convenient situation; it is followed up by a stoppage of wages [Mr Barnard]. *We stop it out of the income monthly, but the man has a power of appeal* [Mr Pease]. *He can appeal to the directors* [Mr Barnard]. *There is very little difficulty; they are very orderly generally.'*

The Railway Archives at York contain many examples of the management notices that were pinned up at Shildon Works during the 1840's. They give some idea of the more common abuses and offences against discipline and of the constant threat of dismissal, short-time, and reduction in wages under which the men lived.

June 12, 1840

No footings[2] allowed in these Works; any person who is known to demand or receive a footing will be considered as giving a month's notice of his discharge.

November 23, 1840

No more overtime to be worked in this Establishment, without special orders, until further notice.

December 23, 1840

Every workman employed in these Works, is informed that he is engaged for a term of One Month or 4 Weeks, and any one quitting this employ before the expiration of that term will have no wages due to him.

No workman will be paid off, without giving or receiving a month's or 4 weeks' notice of his discharge; such notice to expire at the end of a Calendar Month.

Any Person leaving the Works for the day, and not leaving his Time-board, will lose his time for that day; and every person is to enter on his Time-board the Number of the Engine or Engines, he has been at work upon during the day.

January 4, 1841

Key-board. In future no excuse will be taken for any Workman's not leaving his Key upon the Key-board, when he quits work for the day.

December 1, 1841

A general reduction of Wages will take place in these Works to commence January 1st, 1842.[3]

October 10, 1842

On and after Monday, the 17th of this Month, the Workman employed at this establishment to work only 8 daytime, that is, to leave off at 3½ o'clock in the afternoon on Saturday the ¾ day to close at 12 o'clock.

The Managers wish the Workmen to understand that they feel themselves obliged either to dismiss many of the hands or to shorten the time; they have preferred the latter as less injurious to the men generally.

February 28, 1845

A general advance in Wages will take place in this establishment to commence next Month. It must be understood that it will not affect every workman; only those whose present rate of wages and workmanship will justify it.

June 3, 1846

Complaint having been made that the Enginemen are much interrupted by persons, chiefly the workmen of this Establishment, getting on the Locomotive Engines as they pass the works, the Workmen are hereby requested entirely to desist from so doing.

November 26, 1846

The men engaged at these works are desired to refrain from taking firewood or shavings from any part of the premises, but may take them from the chip house except during working hours. Children are not allowed to take any firewood.

June 10, 1847

Arrangement made to refund sum of money (2d. each for those who pay 3d., 1d. each for those who pay 2d.) for children of employees—for education—so long as the child's attendance at school is guaranteed.

November 1, 1847

From this date there will be allowed for Brass and Copper cuttings and turnings at the rate of 1d. per lb.

A general reduction of wages will take place next month, throughout the works[4]

February 18, 1848

The following order in paying the men will be strictly observed, and no man to leave his work before that division in which he is employed shall be sent for:

1st Labourers and wagon wrights

2nd Joiners and Pattern Makers, Painters and Brassfounders

3rd Boiler Smiths

4th Smiths

5th Fitters and Cleaners

Any man living at a distance from the village and being desirous of having his pay earlier, is requested to apply through his Foreman during the earlier part of the day and he will be sent for.

April 19, 1848

T O O L S - Notice is hereby given to the workmen of this establishment that anyone getting Tools from the Tool-keepers is considered responsible for the delivery of such Tools in perfect order and condition back to the Tool-keeper from whom they were obtained—and in no case shall any workman be excused for handing the Tools over to his fellow workman instead of to the Tool-keeper. Any neglect of this notice will be visited with fine or dismissal as circumstances may influence the judgement of the Managers.

May 29, 1848

In consequence of the great irregularity and inaccuracy which at present exists in the workmen's time-boards, the workmen are informed that anyone bringing in other than his own board will from the 1st of June be fined or dismissed as circumstances may influence. Any workman neglecting to bring in his board will forfeit that day's wages upon which such neglect occurs.

The Company had to watch every penny. There was nothing to spare. In 1858, for instance, the Works was closed to commemorate the death of Edward Pease. The funeral was held at the Friends' Meeting House in Darlington and employees at Shildon were allowed free passes for the special train. The time lost, however, had to be made up by unpaid over-time-working on four evenings during the following week.[5]

Stealing and misuse of materials were pounced on and the culprits publicly branded. A typical notice, signed by the Manager, William Bouch, is dated 28 September 1855 and is worded as follows:

It is reported to Me that you are in the habit of Carrying lumps of Coke & Coal home at night and it is suspected that such lumps are taken from truck wagons on the line. Such proceeding is very damaging to your character & quite a disgrace to men in Your position. I hope this notice will be a sufficient caution to prevent a recurrence of such improper conduct—if however you are reported to me again you may expect that it will be attended with very serious results.

Names	CHAS. BAXTER	GEORGE THOMPSON
	THOS. COULSON	WM. GLADDERS
	JAS. COULSON	
	MATT. PATTERSON	
	SIMPSON GLADDERS	
	PIP BENNISON	

The most dramatic instance of the discipline enforced by Bouch is perhaps one reflected in a notice of 23 July 1862. It reads:

Any Workman or Apprentice found using cotton waste in the privies will be discharged.

The Shildon records are unusually full. They give a very good picture of a tough, well-managed working-community in an area where jobs were hard to come by and where the men had to accept the employer's conditions. There are a number of letters, mostly written during the 1840's, in which men plead with the Board for more money. On 26 April 1842, for example, William Cranford wrote saying his wages of 14s. a week were 'insufficient to maintain my riseing family', and begged for 'promotion to anything that is likely to add to wages'; while on 25 June 1841, a man who had been offered a clerical job at Shildon declined it in these terms, in a letter to the Chairman and Committee of the Stockton and Darlington Railway Company:

Gentlemen, After due consideration of the nature & duties of the situation at Darn Depot, & the candid Explanation kindly given me by Mr Pease on Friday last, I cannot conceive it possible that the very limited Salary named can be made by any Means adequate to the support of a little Family, & the close Application for so many Hours per day precludes all chance of making any addition to the Income by other means; in consequence of which I must most respectfully (altho' with reluctance) Beg leave to decline it & with every feeling of Gratitude to you, Gentlemen, & my kind friend R. Flaunders, Esq. must remain . . .[6]

One should, however, stress that the railways were by no means bad employers by the standards of their time. They recruited and employed staff in a labour market which, by modern standards, was both harsh and wasteful. In general men were taken on and turned off with little regard for the consequences to them and their families, although then, as now, it was a remarkably foolish employer who failed to do everything possible to hold on to highly skilled men, if only to prevent them from going to a competitor.[7]

Jobs with the railway companies were, from the beginning, greatly sought after. They offered a degree of security which had previously been almost unknown to working-class families. The welfare arrangements, too, were highly attractive to people who were exceedingly familiar with the disastrous financial consequences of accidents and illness.

The Rules of the Great Western, Bristol and Exeter and South Wales Railways Provident Society, issued in 1885,[8] show clearly the advantages of railway employment. The railwayman belonged to a privileged class of workers. On joining the Provident Society, he had to be between 18 and 35 years of age, and in good health. To obtain a benefit of £1 a week during illness, a man of 20 paid 8½d. into the fund. A man of 45 paid 1s. 6d. In exchange for their contributions, benefit was payable for 26 weeks, as a continuous period.

'No member', said the Rules, 'shall receive any sick allowance whose disability has been occasioned by, or arisen from quarrelling, fighting or drunkenness, or by being engaged in any unlawful act, or by joining in any riot, or by the venereal disease.'[9]

There was a 'death allowance' of up to £12, paid to the member's family, and of up to £6 for the death of the member's wife. Anyone certified as permanently unable to work was entitled to a pension of up to 14s. a week. In case of illness, medical expenses were also paid, in addition to the sickness allowance. On leaving the Company, a man could get a third of his contribution refunded to him.

The 1854 Rules for the London and South-Western Friendly Society were very similar, except for this provision: 'contributions to cease at the age of sixty-five, when the retiring member will receive half-pay for the remainder of his life.'

The railways were notable pioneers of social welfare, in arranging for contributory benefits, employing doctors, building and running hospitals and convalescent homes and providing libraries and educational schemes, in an age where these things were rarities. They were able to finance these enterprises because they employed such large numbers of men. No previous employing body had been responsible for so many people. The railwayman had security, as well as prestige, as a result of belonging to a large organisation. The men in the railway workshops benefitted from the existence of the thousands of drivers, foremen, signalmen, guards and other members of the operating staff. They could be severely disciplined because their jobs were worth holding.

Working men have a strongly developed instinct for self preservation. Unless they are seriously misled or misinformed, they usually act prudently, because they have a great deal to lose. It is easy to understand why railway employees were reluctant to join Trade Unions. The railways in Britain began operations in what, from the employers' point of view, was very much a sellers' market. After 1815 and the end of the Napoleonic wars the arable acreage of the country declined sharply and with it the number of people the farmers needed to employ. There was rural distress as a result, clearly and angrily recorded by Cobbett, culminating in the risings of 1830. The Poor Law of 1834 provided relief for the old, and the jobless, but only on condition that the unfortunates concerned should live in a workhouse, with husbands and wives separated. The Poor Law affected mainly the country districts, but there was widespread unemployment and suffering in the industrial areas between 1836 and 1842, the worst years of the century for the working classes, with jobs hard to get and wages cut to the bone. It was no accident that Chartism, the organised attempt of working people to rise above the poverty level, should have started in 1838 and no accident that in the 1830's and 1840's attempts to form Trade Unions should have been so widely and successfully butchered by the courts. Since 1824, when the notorious combination Acts were repealed, it had been theoretically legal to organise Unions and to belong to them, but the magistrates and judges found no great difficulty in discovering ways round the law.

The great period of railway building and railway investment coincided with the years when the conditions of the working classes were at their worst. One could summarise the situation in this way:

New capital invested in railways			
1826-30	£4 million	1830	Agricultural risings
1831-35	£15 million	1834	Poor Law
1836-40	£48 million	1838-42	Chartism
1840-46	£87 million	1847-48	Great depression in trade, with further mass-unemployment.

It is quite possible that the huge amounts of capital which poured into the railways during the second quarter of the nineteenth century were at the expense of manufacturing industry and that, in this sense, the railways were a major cause of the failure of industry to grow fast enough and steadily enough to provide work for the rising population. From this point of view—the workers' point of view—the railways played an oddly mixed role in the national economy. On the one hand they were to be welcomed, because they provided regular work for many thousands of men and because the new transport system made it much easier for industry to develop, but on the other hand they were to be feared and hated, because they absorbed too high a proportion of the nation's capital over a relatively short, but critical period, and because they abused their strength and prestige as an employer to impose a discipline which went far beyond what the actual conditions required, and which was kept going for much too long. To some extent this was the fault of the Trade Unions themselves. By 1910 there were five unions, usually at loggerheads with one another, to represent the men on the operating side. In the workshops this fragmentation was even worse, with no fewer than 47 different unions competing for members. It was a situation which suited the railway management very well and which understandably they were not reluctant to turn to their own advantage.

A NUMBER of Acts regulating conditions in factories were passed during the nineteenth century. The first of these Acts was drawn up to remedy flagrant abuses and dealt mainly with the employment of children. Until the 1870's no attempt was made to legislate on a more comprehensive scale. The pioneering Act, long before the coming of railways, was in 1802. It was entitled 'An Act for the preservation of the health and morals of apprentices and others employed in cotton and other mills and cotton and other factories'. In 1833 the employment of children under the age of nine was forbidden by a second Act. This contained other important provisions dealing with hours and conditions of employment of children and persons under eighteen years of age. It was followed by a number of other Acts throughout the century.

It was not until 1878 that an attempt was made to consolidate the somewhat chaotic provisions of the previous Acts. The new Act, the Factory and Workshop Act, 1878, repealed the whole of the previous legislation (with the curious exception of the Steam Whistles Act, 1872), and dealt for the first time in a comprehensive way with the conditions of employment in factories and workshops.

It was a long Act, containing important sections relating to sanitary provision, safety and working hours. A factory or workshop, said one of its clauses, 'shall be kept in a cleanly state and free from effluvia arising from any drain, privy or other nuisance'. Machinery had to be fenced and cleaning was not to be carried out while a machine was in motion, or by a 'child, young person or woman'. Working hours were to be either 6 a.m. to 6 p.m. or 7 a.m. to 7 p.m., with a total of 2 hours a day for meals. There could be permission for special working hours for women and young people in factories driven by water-power.

Special arrangements for ventilation had to be made in any part of a factory where conditions might be especially dangerous to health. A grinding department, for instance, would be placed in this category. Accidents had to be reported to the Inspectors, who were given full powers to enter any building at any time and to talk to any person employed there.

Article 78 laid down: 'There shall be affixed at the entrance to a factory and a workshop, and in such other parts thereof as an inspector for the time being directed and in such position as to be easily read by the person employed in the factory or workshop.

(1) A prescribed abstract of this Act . . .

(5) Every notice and document required by this Act to be affixed in the factory or workshop.'

The railway workshops were, of course, subject to this Act, as they had been to the relevant sections of its predecessors. They also had to observe the provisions of the Truck Acts, and their rules and regulations in the latter part of the nineteenth century were affected in several important ways by them.

The first Truck Act was passed in 1831. Thereafter employers had to be careful how they paid their men. Under Section 1 of the Act they were instructed that 'in contracts for the hiring of artificers, wages shall be made payable in current coin'; under Section 2 that 'no stipulations shall be inserted as to the manner in which wages shall be expended'; and under Section 3 that payment in goods was illegal. Agreed deductions from wages were allowed to be made in respect of tools, rent and food.

The 1831 Act was lacking in precision on one important point, which had to be clarified in subsequent Acts. It left considerable doubt as to whether it was legal to make deductions for fines, a practice which was common among most of, if not all, the railway companies. This was tested several times in the courts and the new Truck Act of 1896 was more specific. The relevant section reads:

DEDUCTIONS ON PAYMENTS IN RESPECT OF FINES

1. An employer shall not make any contract with any workman for any deduction from the sum contracted to be paid by the employer to the workman, for or in respect of any fine, unless

   (a) the terms of the contract are contained in a notice kept constantly affixed to such place or places open to the workmen and in such a position that it may be easily seen, read, and copied by any person whom it affects; or the contract is in writing, signed by the workman, and

   (b) the contract specifies the acts or omissions in respect of which the

fine may be imposed, and the amount of the fine or the particulars from which that amount may be ascertained; and
(c) the fine imposed under the contract is in respect of some act or omission which causes or is likely to cause damage or loss to the employer, or interruption or hindrance to his business.
(d) the amount of the fine is fair and reasonable having regard to all the circumstances of the case.
2. An employer shall not make any such deduction or receive any such payment unless
(a) the deduction or payment is made in pursuance of, or in accordance with, such a contract as aforesaid; and
(b) particulars in writing showing the acts or omissions in respect of which the fine is imposed and the amount thereof are supplied to the workman on each occasion where a deduction of payment is made.

Domestic servants were specifically omitted from the Truck Act of 1831. They were also excluded from the Employers and Workmen Act of 1875, and from the Truck Amendment Act, 1887.

It was almost certainly due to the Truck Act of 1896 that the railway companies began the habit of issuing all their employees, both in the workshops and on the operating side, with a book of rules which had to be signed as evidence of their agreement to the conditions of service, which, in a number of cases, included the power to fine a man a fixed amount for a particular offence. By signing his rule book, a railwayman gave his employer permission to fine him and to deduct fines from his wages.

A printed poster, relating to the Truck Act, was issued at Derby on 18 June 1897[1] above the signature of the General Manager of the Midland Railway, John Mathieson. It appears to refer only to the members of the operating staff.

In accordance with the Truck Act, 1896, Notice is hereby given, that the Company reserve the right to impose the following fines in respect of the acts or omissions mentioned below, and to deduct from the wages of their servants, and to retain the sums that may be imposed as fines.

2/6d. 1. For inattention whilst on duty, absence from duty without leave, coming late on duty, leaving duty before proper time or before being relieved, coming on duty without proper rest, or otherwise unfit for duty, permitting relief by men unauthorised or unfit for duty.

2/6d. 2. For insubordination or non-observance of the lawful orders of a superior officer, or for the use of abusive or offensive language whilst on duty, or for the wilful misrepresentation or suppression of facts in a verbal or written report, or for failing to report irregularities or accidents.

2/6d. 3. For incivility or want of proper courtesy or attention to Passengers or other members of the public.

5/0d.   4. For negligence or misconduct by which damage or delay is,
          or may be, caused to trains or traffic.
5/0d.   5. For negligence or misconduct by which loss is, or may be,
          caused to the Company, or by which damage or injury is, or
          may be, caused to luggage, parcels, animals, goods or traffic,
          or to engines, vehicles, machines, signals, lamps or other
          property of the Company.
10/-   6. For negligence or misconduct whereby danger or risk of
          danger is, or may be, caused to human life.
      For a repetition of any of the above offences, the fine may be doubled.

In drawing up rules for the men employed in their workshops, the railways followed the ordinary industrial practice of the period. Fining for
misdemeanours was a normal method of discipline, and the size of the
fines, in relation to the wage-rates in force, must have been a powerful
deterrent. The railways were remarkable only in the number of men they
employed and in the prestige of a railway job.

   To provide an opportunity of comparing the rules of the railway
workshops with those drawn up for other industrial establishments, two
mid-nineteenth century examples of the latter are given below. One is
for a large concern, the Frodingham Iron Works in Lincolnshire, and the
other for the Bratton Iron Works, a small family business near Westbury
in Wiltshire.

   The Frodingham rules were:

HOURS OF WORK

1. The usual hours of work for men on time work to be from six
   o'clock in the morning till six o'clock in the evening, allowing
   half-an-hour for breakfast and an hour for dinner. On Saturdays
   the working day will close at four o'clock.
2. The hours of work for shift workmen to be one week from six
   o'clock in the morning until six o'clock in the evening, and the
   other week from six o'clock in the evening until six o'clock in the
   morning, alternately.
3. The bell will be rung for work at six, nine, and one o'clock. Workmen who are not later than fifteen minutes after the first bell, or
   five minutes after either of the others, shall be allowed to commence work. This privilege to be forfeited at the discretion of the
   masters should the workmen take undue advantage of it.

WAGES AND RULES

4. The wages to be paid fortnightly, on Saturday, when the workmen
   will be paid for their time or work done up to the previous Saturday
   night.
5. Each workman on obtaining employment at the works must
   procure from the office a copy of these rules, which he will also have
   to sign.

TIME BOARDS

6. Each workman on entering the works will be supplied with a time-board on which to enter his time, subject to the following restrictions.

   First—Should he commence work without taking his board from the office, he will lose his time so wrought.

   Second—Should he omit to leave his time-board at the office when done work, he will be liable to lose his time for that day.

   Third—He will not be paid for any time that is not entered on his time-board.

7. No workman will be allowed to take out or put in the time-board of another workman. A breach of this rule will subject him to a fine at the discretion of the masters for the first offence, and to dismissal on a repetition of such offence.

8. Each workman on shift work must enter the shifts so wrought on his time board, in the same manner as if he were on day work.

9. Each workman on piece work must enter his piece work on his time-board, in the same manner as if he were on day work.

10. Any workman taking a shift for another man must enter the name on a time-board, stating the name of the man whose shift he has worked.

11. Each workman must keep for himself a daily check-board of his time, so that in case of his disputing the office account, it can be produced and compared with the time book. Unless such a check-board is kept, the workman must in all cases take the office account.

12. Every workman must, on the Saturday previous to the pay Saturday, enter on his time-board his total time for the past fortnight.

PIECE WORK

13. Men working piece work, whether directly or under another contractor, are to be subject to and bound by all the same rules as those who work by time.

TIME AND PIECE WORK

14. Any labourer or other workman who shall be sent by the foreman to assist a piece workman shall do so, under penalty of immediate dismissal if he refuse, provided the wages paid to him are not less than those he is earning on time.

STORES

15. No workman will be allowed to obtain anything from the storehouse without a written order from his foreman.

SMITHS

16. Each smith, whether on piece or day work, will be required to enter on his slate (daily) the description and weight of the articles he makes, and the purpose for which each article is intended to be used.

TOOLS

17. Any workman taking the tools of another workman without his permission will subject himself to a fine, as each workman is considered responsible for the tools entrusted to him.

INTOXICATING LIQUORS

18. Any workman bringing intoxicating liquors of any description into the works will be subject to instant dismissal.

FOOTINGS

19. Footings or fees of any kind are strictly prohibited.

NOTICE OF LEAVING

20. Notice in writing must be given by any workman on a pay day fourteen days previous to his leaving his employment, under penalty of the forfeiture of a week's wages; similar notice will be given to each workman previous to his being discharged, the masters reserving the right of immediate dismissal in case of insubordination or gross misconduct.
21. In case of the dismissal of a workman for insubordination or misconduct, he shall not be entitled to receive his wages until the pay day next ensuing.

DAMAGE TO EMPLOYERS' PROPERTY

22. Any workman damaging the machinery or property of his employer, either through carelessness or design, shall be fined twenty shillings.

SLAG BOGIE THROWN OVER TIP

23. In case of a slag bogie being thrown over the tip, both driver and tipper to be fined two shillings and sixpence each, unless they give a good and sufficient reason for the accident.

LEAVE OF ABSENCE

24. Unless he gives six hours' notice at the office of his being unable to come, any workman, whether on time work, shift work, or piece work, who is not ready to start his work at the proper time, will be fined ten shillings for the first offence, twenty shillings for the second, and for the third be liable to immediate dismissal, a fine of twenty shillings being in that case stopped off any wages due to him at that time.
25. If, however, it should appear that there has not been a satisfactory reason for his thus being absent from work, he will render himself liable to the penalties under rule 20.

CHANGE OF SHIFTS

26. No workman to leave the works until the man who has to change shifts with him has come. Any workman coming late to be reported by the man who has been kept waiting.

HOIST, ENGINE HOUSES, &c

27. Any man riding on either hoist cage will be dismissed.
28. No workman is allowed to be in any of the engine houses except on business.

DISMISSAL

29. The employers reserve to themselves the right of dismissing the offender, in addition to his fine; and it is also in their option, for any breach of the above rules, to bring the offender before the magistrates.

CLUB

30. All workmen employed on the works to be members of the Frodingham Iron Works Doctor's Club.

HOUSES

31. Any workman occupying or residing in any of the houses belonging to the masters, shall, at the expiration of his notice, be bound to leave the same, and shall not be entitled to receive his pay until he delivers the keys of such house at the office.

IMPROPER LANGUAGE

32. The workmen are strictly cautioned against the use of profane or improper language, and the masters earnestly request them carefully to abstain from a practice so degrading to themselves and so offensive to others.
33. The object of these rules being to increase the comfort and respectability of the workmen, as well as the good order of the establishment, it is hoped they will be carefully observed.

At the end, there were spaces for the date and the new employee's signature. The preceding sentence read: 'I, the undersigned, do hereby certify that in consideration of wages to be paid to me as they become due, I have entered the employment of Messrs THE FRODINGHAM IRON CO., subject to the above Rules, of which I have received a copy, as witness my hand . . .'

The copy in my possession is signed by Thomas Berry and dated 24 February 1866.

The Bratton Iron Works was run by R. and J. Reeves and Son. It had grown out of a small blacksmith's business and by the middle of the nineteenth century it was the main employer of labour in the village after agriculture, making and repairing most of the agricultural implements.

The rules were agreed to in 1871 and printed. They contain a number of delightful items:

I   The time for working shall be Fifty-six hours in a week, viz. Five days of Ten hours each, and Six hours on Saturday. During the months of October, November, December, January, February and March, work shall commence on each day at Half-past Six o'clock in the Morning, and leave off work at Six o'clock in the Evening. During the months of April, May, June, July, August and September, work will commence at Six o'clock in the Morning, and leave off work at Half-past Five o'clock in the Evening. On Saturdays work shall commence at Half-past Six o'clock in the Morning all the year round, and leave off work at Quarter-past One o'clock. The Meal hours shall be for Breakfast from Half-past Eight until Quarter-past Nine, and for Dinner from Quarter-past One until Two o'clock.

II   Any Workman whether at Day Work or at Piece Work late in the Morning or at either Meal Time shall be fined the amount of Half-an-hour's Time unless there is a reason for his being late satisfactory to his Masters. The Whistle shall be blown exactly at time for working, and all persons not on the premises at the time will be considered as late.

III   All persons shall enter the premises in the morning and at meal times by the Lower Gates opposite the Office, and any person entering the premises to commence work by another way shall be fined Threepence for each offence.

IV   No time shall be allowed for Luncheon or Tea to any person during the hours of work, any person breaking this Rule shall be fined according to Rule XIV.

V   An interval of Fifteen Minutes will be stopped for Tea, for those Workmen working Over-time, but such time for Tea shall be at the close of the day's work, viz. Half-past Five or Six o'clock as the case may be, and all persons shall commence work punctual at the close of the fifteen minutes or they will be liable to be fined the same as at other meal times.

VI   All persons shall be paid by the Hour according to the time worked in each week.

VII   Any person overstating his time shall be fined twice the amount of the time so overstated.

VIII   Any person Idling or Wasting his Time shall be fined for each offence Sixpence.

IX   Any person requiring Beer they shall bring it in at the Meal Time, and at no other time shall Beer be allowed to be brought on to the premises.

X   No person shall bring in more than One pint at a meal time, and each person shall bring their own separately.

XI   Any person found bringing Beer or Intoxicating Liquors on the works, except at the meal time, or bringing more than allowed by the above rules shall be fined One Shilling for each offence.

XII   Any person leaving his work at any time to go to the Public House or any place for the purpose of getting Beer, shall be fined One Shilling for each offence.

XIII Any person coming on the premises in a state of Intoxication shall be fined One Shilling.

XIV Any person leaving, neglecting or absenting himself from his work at any time when he is required to be at work, without having first obtained permission, shall be fined Sixpence for each offence unless he can give a satisfactory reason to his Masters as to the cause of his absence.

XV Any person cursing, or swearing an oath, or using obscene or profane language on the works, shall be fined One Shilling.

XVI Any person throwing at another, or interrupting another in his work or in any way causing any annoyance to his fellow workmen shall be fined Threepence.

XVII Any person found damaging any Article or Machine, either wilfully or carelessly, shall be fined sufficient to replace the same.

XVIII Any person waisting [sic] Materials, in any way, shall be fined Sixpence.

XIX Any person making any Tools, or doing any work for themselves, or taking away any kind of Materials, Firewood, or Shavings off the premises without having first obtained permission from the Masters shall be fined for each offence One Shilling.

XX Any person leaving his Lamp or Candle burning after leaving work shall be fined Threepence.

XXI No Smoking shall be allowed at any time on the premises, any person so doing shall be fined Sixpence for each offence.

XXII No person shall be allowed to send Boys off the premises on any business of their own, any person so doing shall pay the fine instead of the Boy according to Rule XIV.

XXIII All Workmen before leaving shall give One Week's Notice of his intention to do so on the Saturday previous, and in like manner all Workmen shall recieve [sic] One Week's Notice from the Masters before being discharged excepting for improper conduct to the Masters or Officials, for such they will be liable to Instant Dismissal.

XXIV Any person knowing another break any of the above Rules, and do not inform his Masters of it, shall be liable to be fined an equal fine same as the offenders.

All Fines before mentioned will be deducted from the Wages and will be appropriated to the Sick Fund for the Benefit of the Workmen.

These Rules were agreed on by the Masters and Workmen on the Twenty-second day of December, One Thousand Eight Hundred and Seventy-One, and will be binding on all persons employed on the Works, but the Masters may be at liberty to reduce the amount of fine in the case of Boys or Apprentices as they may think fit.

The Frodingham and Bratton rules both display a characteristic which is missing from the railway rule books. They are firmly paternalistic in tone, whereas the railway managements were always, for

C

some reason, much colder and more outspokenly authoritarian. One cannot imagine the Great Western Railway 'earnestly requesting' its employees 'carefully to abstain from a practice so degrading to themselves and so offensive to others', or assuring them that the object of the rules was 'to increase the comfort and respectability of the workmen'. Nor can we think of the railway works at Swindon or Crewe as one big family, with each member responsible for the conduct of the others. The last clause of the Bratton agreement, 'any person knowing another break any of the above rules, and do not inform his Masters of it, shall be liable to be fined an equal fine same as the offenders', would have been impossible in a railway works.

The difference must be partly a product of size, but even more, perhaps, of the peculiar circumstances under which the railways and their workshops were built and developed. The Frodingham and Bratton Iron Works grew up gradually, so that a tradition was established over the years, and paternalism was possible, if not inevitable. The railways, on the other hand, had to set themselves up rapidly from nothing and recruit large staffs from any sources that were available. Something of the rough and ready discipline imposed on the gangs who built the railways may have spilled over into their later operation.[2] It is possible that only autocrats could have got the railways going in the first place and nurtured them through their first few decades of growth. Paternalism certainly became a feature of railway management later in the century, especially in towns where the railway company was the only or the principal employer, but it was paternalism infused into an earlier autocratic system, rather than thorough-going paternalism. The difference is an important one.

4

CONTROLLING THE WORKERS
AT SWINDON

THE most comprehensive system of fines seems to have been instituted by the Great Western Railway in their Swindon works.[1] The 1904 revision[2] of the Swindon rule book, containing details of their fines, is a lengthy document. It has thirty-nine sections and is headed

Rules and Regulations to be observed by workmen employed in the Workshops of the Locomotive, Carriage and Wagon Departments

1. Every applicant for employment must be in good health and will only be temporarily engaged until a satisfactory character has been received from his last employer for whom he has worked six months. He must produce his Certificate of Birth, and must sign a declaration that he has read a copy of these Rules, and that he undertakes to observe and be bound by them as a condition of his employment.

CONDITIONS OF SERVICE

2. The usual hours of work are as follows: —

Monday to Friday
$\begin{cases} \text{6 a.m. to 8.15 a.m.} \\ \text{9 a.m. to 1.00 p.m.} \\ \text{2 p.m. to 5.30 p.m.} \end{cases}$

Saturdays
$\begin{cases} \text{6 a.m. to 8.15 a.m.} \\ \text{9 a.m. to 12 noon} \end{cases}$

totalling 54 hours per week, or an average of nine hours per day. Overtime will be reckoned after 5.30

HOURS OF WORK

35

p.m. each day, except Saturday, when it will be reckoned after 12 noon. It will be valued at the rate of time and a half after that hour. This clause applies only to men who have worked the full number of hours during the day. Men not regularly employed on Sunday duty will be paid for Sunday work at the rate of time and a half.

No overtime will be allowed until 54 hours per week have been made, except when work is stopped by reason of accidents to machinery, or when a man has, under pressure of work, worked all the previous night, or when the works are closed at holiday times: Sunday work to stand by itself.

Gas-makers, Furnace-men and others, whose working hours do not correspond with this rule, will be paid according to arrangements made to suit the circumstances of each case.

3. Every workman is required, as a Condition of Service, to become a member of the G.W.R. Medical Fund Society, for providing medicines and medical service for the members and their families, and a member of the G.W.R. Sick Fund Society, unless he is already in Benefit Societies which provide adequate benefit in case of sickness. SICK & MEDICAL FUND SOCIETIES

    NOTE: This rule applies to Swindon Works only

4. The engagement is terminable by 9 working hours' notice on either side. In case of misconduct the workman will be liable to instant dismissal. RESIGNATION AND DISMISSAL

5. Any workman absent from the works more than one quarter day, whether from illness or otherwise, must notify the Foreman of the shop, stating the cause of absence. ABSENCE FROM DUTY

    Any workman absent from work for two days without leave, will be considered as having left the Service, as from the commencement of the absence.

Any workman absent through lead poisoning must at once inform his Foreman, so that the case may be reported to H.M. Factory Inspector.

6. Each workman will be provided with a number which will be stamped on the metal ticket, or time-recording card supplied. He must place the ticket in the box provided for the purpose each time he enters the Works. Workmen who are required to record their time by Time Recorders must strictly observe the instructions laid down for the use of these machines.

TIME TICKETS AND TIME RECORDERS

Any workman having lost or mislaid his ticket can have his time booked by reporting the matter to the ticket man before the box is closed, but a charge of 6d. will be made for a new ticket. Any workman being present at the commencement of a period of work, and failing to book his time, may have his time booked, provided he can, during the period of work, prove to the satisfaction of his Foreman that he was present at its commencement, and will be liable to a fine of 6d. Any workman putting in a ticket other than his own, or tampering with the Time Recorder, will be liable to instant dismissal.

7. Each workman must enter in the book or time sheet provided for the purpose, the name and description of the work on which he has been employed during the previous day, and if on more than one job, the time on each. Any workman neglecting to enter the time correctly, or to deposit the book or sheet at the proper time and place, will be liable to a fine of 6d.

TIME BOOKS AND TIME SHEETS

8. The cash boxes in which the wages are paid must be deposited in the box provided for their collection before 9

CASH BOXES

o'clock on the Monday morning
following the pay. Any workman neglecting to do this will be liable to a
fine of 6d.

9. Any workman found playing, idling
or quarrelling during working hours
will be liable to a fine of 2s. 6d. and,
in the event of an accident occurring
through such misconduct, the workman in default must pay any or all
expenses to which the Company may
be put.

QUARRELLING,
IDLING, &c

10. Any workman leaving off work or
washing without proper authority
before the hooter sounds, or washing
his hands in oil, will be liable to a
fine of 1s. for each offence.

CEASING WORK
BEFORE HOOTER
SOUNDS AND
UNAUTHORISED
WASHING

11. Any workman leaving or entering the
premises by any other way than the
doors appointed will be liable to instant dismissal.

LEAVING OR
ENTERING WORKS

12. Any workman leaving the works
during working hours, without permission, will forfeit his wages from
the commencement of that period of
the day, and be liable to a fine of 1s.
in addition, no one will be allowed at
any time to take out of the works any
tool or material unless authorized by
a pass from his Foreman, which must
state the number of the pieces. No
workman, except those providing
their own tools, is allowed to carry
any basket or parcel into the works,
but must leave it with the attendants
in the Mess Room. All passes must
be left with the gate-keeper, who is
required to take account of material
of any kind taken out of the works.

LEAVING WORKS
DURING WORKING
HOURS, AND
TAKING OUT
MATERIAL

13. Every workman will be held responsible for the tools entrusted to him,
and he will be required to see that
the initials of the Company, as well
as his own private mark, are upon
them, or be liable to a fine of 1s.

TOOLS

14. A workman borrowing tools from
another must return them, and in
the event of their being lost or

BORROWING
TOOLS

damaged may be called upon to pay their value.

15. Every workman must provide himself with such personal tools as are usual in his trade, and must insure them; the Company will not be responsible for any such tools which may be destroyed or injured by fire.

PERSONAL TOOLS TO BE INSURED

16. A workman using taps, dies, rimers, or other general tools, must see that they are returned in good condition to the person appointed to take charge of them, or he will be liable to a fine of 2s. 6d.

TAPS, DIES, RIMERS, &c

17. Any workman making a tool without instructions from his Foreman, will be liable to a fine of 2s. 6d., or instant dismissal.

UNAUTHORISED MAKING OF TOOLS

18. For every drilling, planing, or nut cutting machine, the prescribed lubricant must be used. A workman using oil without being specially ordered to do so by his Foreman, will be liable to a fine of 1s. Dirty or greasy waste must not be left lying around, but must be placed in the receptacle for such material.

LUBRICANTS AND DIRTY WASTE

19. A workman using a machine or other article improperly, or damaging it through neglect, shall pay the amount of the damage, and be liable to instant dismissal.

DAMAGE TO MACHINERY, &c

20. A workman making use of any material which is cracked or otherwise unfit for the purpose for which it is intended, will be liable to a fine of 2s. 6d., or to instant dismissal.

USE OF IMPROPER MATERIAL

21. A workman making an article of wrong dimensions, or finishing work in an inferior or unworkmanlike manner, may be called upon to make good such work, and be liable to a fine of 2s. 6d. or to instant dismissal.

INFERIOR WORKMANSHIP

22. A workman leaving the service of the Company, will not be paid his wages until he delivers up the key of his drawer or tool chest, and the

HANDING IN OF KEYS BEFORE LEAVING SERVICE

tools entrusted to him, to the satisfaction of the person authorized to
receive them.

23. Smiths and Strikers will not be
allowed to fetch in slack or coals to
their fires, excepting where men are
not specially appointed for that
purpose.

SMITHS AND
STRIKERS NOT
TO FETCH COAL

24. Where men are not specially appointed for the duty, Smiths are required to see that their fires are put
out every night before leaving, and
that the blast is shut off, or be liable
to a fine of 2s. 6d.

SMITHS TO
EXTINGUISH FIRES

25. Where men are not specially appointed for the duty, every workman
must shut off the gas or put out the
lights he has been using, before
going to meals or leaving off work, or
he will be liable to a fine of 1s.

GAS LIGHTS &c
TO BE EXTINGUISHED

26. A workman who goes into a workshop
in which he is not usually employed,
except by the order of his Foreman,
will be liable to a fine of 2s. 6d.

WORKMEN NOT TO
ENTER SHOPS
OTHER THAN
THEIR OWN

27. A workman who brings intoxicating
liquor into the works will be liable to
instant dismissal.[3]

INTOXICATING
LIQUOR

28. A workman who smokes in the workshops, or within the precincts of the
works, will be liable to a fine of 2s. 6d.

SMOKING

29. All Stores required must be obtained
from the Storekeeper by an order
signed by the Foreman of the shop.
If any brass or other material is lost,
the workman in charge of the same
will be held responsible, and if no
satisfactory account can be given,
he will be liable to a fine of 2s. 6d., or
to instant dismissal.

STORES

30. A workman who breaks open another
workman's drawer or box, or any box
containing tools belonging to a lathe
or other piece of machinery, will be
liable to a fine of 2s. 6d. or to instant
dismissal.
A workman who locks up any drill,
brace or other general tool, or tools
belonging to any piece of machinery

BREAKING OPEN
DRAWERS, BOXES
&c.

(unless he is working constantly at that machine), will be liable to a fine of 2s. 6d. or to instant dismissal.

31. The moving parts of any Engine, Crane, Lathe, or other machine, must not be oiled or cleaned while in motion. The legs, beds, and frames may be cleaned during the week, but the other parts on Saturdays only, when 15 minutes will be allowed for cleaning a single lathe or machine, and 20 minutes for a crank lathe, a double-headed lathe, or two machines. The parts of a lathe or machine must not be changed while in motion. No workman must attempt to put on a strap or interfere with the main shafting in any way while the engine is in motion.

A workman who violates any provision of this rule will be considered guilty of serious and wilful misconduct, and to have rendered himself liable to instant dismissal.

CLEANING MACHINERY

32. Sticks and brushes are provided for the purpose of removing drillings, turnings, etc., from the tools of machines, and any workman removing them with his fingers, will be considered guilty of serious and wilful misconduct, and render himself liable to instant dismissal.

REMOVING BORINGS, DRILLINGS, TURNINGS, &c., FROM MACHINERY

33. It is most important that workmen employed on lathes and other machines, should wear close fitting jackets.

WEARING OF JACKETS

34. Any workman travelling with a free ticket on this Company's line must give the same up to the Station-Master or Ticket Collector at the end of his journey. No workman may ride upon an Engine without proper authority.

FREE TICKETS

35. The Company, in granting privilege ticket facilities, rely on the co-operation of all their workmen to prevent abuse of the privilege, and to report any irregularity which may

PRIVILEGE TICKETS

come under their notice. Any workman detected transferring an order
or ticket issued, or being privy to
such transfer, will be liable to
instant dismissal and prosecution.

36. Any workman guilty of disobedience   DISOBEDIENCE
to his superiors, or adjudged guilty   AND
of serious misconduct will be liable   MISCONDUCT
to instant dismissal.

37. No workman is allowed to trade   TRADING
whilst in the Company's service.[4]

38. Any workman not able to attend at   INABILITY TO
the pay table, must use the pre-   ATTEND PAY
scribed form countersigned by his   TABLE
Foreman, authorising someone to
receive his money.

39. The term "Workman" in these   DEFINITION OF
Rules include "Women, and "Young   WORKMAN
Persons", as defined in the Factory
and Workshops Act of 1901.

                    BY ORDER

This rule book was still in use, un-amended, until the end of the First
World War, and possibly for several years after that. In 1917 Mr C. W.
Love entered the service of the Great Western Railway as an apprentice
in the Swindon Works. His signed rule book has been preserved by his
family.

It is interesting to combine the regulations of the Factory Act with
those to be found in the Swindon rule book, and to see what kind of
working environment and discipline actually resulted. An excellent description is to be found in Alfred Williams' *Life in a Railway Factory*,
which first appeared in 1915.[5]

Williams, who had been employed at Swindon, noticed and com-
mented on the high incidence of stealing which occurred at the Works.
Among the workmen theft had greatly decreased, but he felt the record
needed straightening in one important respect:

It is not the rank and file alone that are guilty of taking things that do not
belong to them. Some of the principals of the staff have been notoriously
to blame in this respect, as is well-known at the works, though their mis-
deeds are invariably screened and condoned. If one of the managers[6] has
stolen materials worth hundreds of pounds he is reprimanded and allowed
to continue at his post, or at most, he is asked to resign and is afterwards
awarded a pension; but if the workman has purloined an article of a few
pence in value he is dismissed and prosecuted. This is no general statement
but a plain matter of fact.

The Factory Act of 1878 had imposed on employers the duty of making sure that their premises were kept 'in a cleanly state and free from effluvia arising from any drain, privy or other nuisance'. It had not, however, made any order concerning the sanitary facilities themselves, and at Swindon these facilities do not appear to have been all they should have been. Alfred Williams has a famous description of the so-called sanitary blocks, each 'built to meet the requirements of about five hundred workmen'.

These buildings are of a uniform type and are disagreeable places, lacking in sanitary arrangements. There is not the slightest approach to privacy of any kind, no consideration whatever for those who happen to be imbued with a sense of modesty or refinement of feeling. The convenience consists of a long double row of seats, situated back to back, partly divided by brick walls, the whole constructed above a large pit that contains a foot of water which is changed once or twice a day. The seats themselves are merely an iron rail built upon brickwork, and there is no protection. Several times, I have known men to overbalance and fall into the pit. Everything is bold, daring and unnatural. On entering, the naked persons of the men sitting may plainly be seen, and the stench is overpowering. The whole concern is gross and objectionable, filthy, disgusting and degrading. No one that is chaste and modest could bear to expose himself, sitting there with no more decency than obtains among herds of cattle shut up in the winter pen. Consequently, there are many who, though hard-pressed by the exigencies of nature, never use the place. As a result they contract irregularities and complaints of the stomach that remain with them all their lives, and that might easily prove fatal to them. Perhaps this barbarous relic of insanitation may in time be superseded by some system a little more moral and more compatible with human sensibility and refinement.

The manufacturing methods and the administration were old-fashioned and inefficient, and the whole establishment, in Williams' view, was ruled by fear[6].

Every shed has an institution called 'The Black List'. This list is filed in the foreman's office and contains the names of those who have been found guilty of any indiscretion, those who may have made a little bad work, indifferent time-keepers and, naturally, those who have fallen into disfavour with the overseer on any other account, and perhaps the names have been added for no offence at all. When it is intended to include a workman on the list, he is sent for to the office, bullied by the overseer before the clerks and office-boy, and warned as to the future. "I've put you on the black list. You know what that means. The next time, mind, and you're out of it. I give you one more chance."

Not long ago an apprentice—a fine, smart, intellectual youth—was asked by a junior mate to advise him as to a piece of work in the lathe and went to give the required assistance. While thus engaged he was sent for to the office and charged with idling by the overseer. He tried to explain that he was helping his mate, but the foreman would not listen to it. "Put him on the black list", he roared to the clerk. The lad's father, enraged at the treatment meted out to his son, promptly removed him from the works, and sacrificed four or five years of patient and studious toil at his trade. It is

44   *Working to Rule*

useless to continue in the shed when you have been stigmatised with the
"black list". You will never make any satisfactory progress; you had
better seek out another place and make a fresh start in life.

The foreman was king. "He whose opinions are most nearly in agreement
with those of the foreman always thrives best, obtains the highest piecework prices and the greatest day wages, too, while the other is certain to be
but under the ban. In brief, the average overseer dislikes you if you are a
tip-top workman, if you have a good carriage and are well-dressed, if you
are clever and cultivated, if you have friends above the average and are well-
connected, if you are religious or independent, manly, and courageous; and
he tolerates you if you creep about, are rough, ragged, and round-shoul-
dered, a born fool, a toady, a liar, a tale-bearer, an indifferent workman—
no matter what you are as long as you say "sir" to him, are servile and
abject, see and hear nothing, and hold with him in everything he says and
does: that is the way to get on in the factory.

The factory-inspectors appear to have turned a blind eye to the conditions in workshops. Williams himself worked in the forge, where sickness and accidents were frequent:

The first-named may be attributed to the foul air prevailing—the dense
smoke and fumes from the oil forges, and the thick, sharp dust and ashes
from the coal fires. The tremendous noise of the hammers and machinery
and the priming of the boilers have a most injurious effect upon the body as
well as upon the nervous system; it is all intensely painful and wearisome
to the workmen. The most common forms of sickness among the men of
the shed are complaints of the stomach and head, with constipation. These
are the direct result of the gross impurity of the air. Colds are exceptionally
common, and are another result of the bad atmospheric conditions; as soon
as you enter into the smoke and fume you are sure to begin sniffing and
sneezing. The black dust and filth is being breathed into the chest and lungs
every moment. At the weekend one is continuously spitting off the accre-
tion; it will take several days to remove it from the body. As a matter of
fact, the workmen are never clean, except at holiday times. However often
they may wash and bathe themselves, an absence from the shed of several
consecutive days will be necessary in order to effect an evacuation of the
filth from all parts of the system. Even the eyes contain it. No matter how
carefully you wash them at night, in the morning they will be surrounded
with dark rings—fine black dust which has come from them as you lay
asleep.

Reading the Medical Report for the county of Wilts recently I noticed it
was said that greater supervision is exercised over the workshops now than
was the case formerly. From my own knowledge and point of view I should
say there is no such supervision of the factory shops at all; during the
twenty odd years I have worked there I have never once heard of a factory
inspector coming through the shed, unless it were one of the company's
own confidential officials.

The Company operated a ruthless hire-and-fire policy:

Sometimes as many as a hundred men of the same shed have received their
notices of dismissal in one day. The notices are written out upon special
forms and the clerk of the shed, or the office-boy, carried them round to the
men; it is a dramatic moment. Although fully expecting to receive the
dreaded "bit of paper", the men hope against hope; they are quite dazed

when the clerk approaches and hands it to them, for they know full well what it means. The young men may not care a scrap. To them all the world is open. They have plenty of other opportunities; but to those who are subject to illness—contracted on the premises—or who are getting on in life and are becoming old and grey and unfit for further service, it is little less than tragedy. One day's notice is served out to the men; they are quickly removed from the shed and are presently forgotten.

Of the number discharged a great many loiter about the town for several weeks, unable to find any sort of employment. These scatter about among the villages and try to obtain work on the farms; those are assisted by their relatives and kindred in various parts of the country to leave the locality altogether. Some find their way into the workhouse and end their days there, and others develop into permanent loafers and outcasts and beg their food from door to door, picking up stray coppers around the station yard or in the market-place.

In a one-industry town like Swindon, with the dread of unemployment always present, the rule book was not difficult to enforce. The unemployment figures for Swindon in the 1920's and 1930's show how insecure a job in the railway Works was until the war and the introduction of new industries into the town combined to improve the situation.

The railway-town took its full share of the economic depression, as the totals of registered unemployed make clear.

26 July 1926	746
25 July 1927	915
28 July 1930	1073
25 July 1932	3026
26 July 1933	3485

In a situation of this kind, the work-shy or rule-breaking employee was not likely to last long.

Certain details of the Swindon rules are a little difficult to understand, however, even against the industrial background of their time. Why, for instance, was it felt necessary to include such a strong warning against washing one's hands in oil, or against oiling a machine without being specifically ordered to do so by the foreman? The main reason, presumably, was that oil was an expensive commodity, to be husbanded as if it were liquid gold. In the 1850's and 1860's this may well have been true: petroleum refineries were still in their infancy and operated on a very small scale. Oil brought across the Atlantic in barrels was unlikely to be cheap, although, even in the pioneering days, it was a good deal cheaper than vegetable oils. But from 1880 onwards the price of oil had fallen considerably and it seems strange in consequence to find the Great Western still acting as if the date were thirty or forty years earlier. It is an interesting piece of industrial conservatism, prohibition for prohibition's sake.

Might it not have been more intelligent to have kept a bucket of oil in the corner of the shop specially for hand-cleaning ?

One wonders, too, about the rule which laid down that nobody was to leave or enter the premises except by means of the doors appointed. It so happens that Swindon Works was, and still is, surrounded by a very high brick wall, which only a fairly desperate prisoner would have been likely to attempt to scale. Unless wall-climbing was envisaged, there were only two ways of getting in or out of the Works, without involving oneself in a very long walk. One was the legal method, through a tunnel under the railway main line and then past the check-gate and into the road. The other route would have been along the track, by walking half a mile along the main line to Swindon station and then passing the ticket-collector, who was a watchful man, with his own strict rules to follow. It is true that exceptionally daring men, with an abundance of energy, might perhaps have got on or off the line much further away from the Works, either east or west, but a man walking along the track was likely to be noticed, unless it was foggy or very dark. This rule, too, does not seem very realistic.

The severe penalties for bad work—a half-crown fine or instant dismissal—would, one might have thought, have been more likely to produce a neurosis among the workmen, with more bad work as a result, than a raising of standards. It is not unreasonable to punish a man for bad behaviour, but it is, under most conditions, foolish to punish him for unsatisfactory production. He could be tired or not well—most of us are on occasions—and it is a singularly unenlightened management which penalises employees for being tired or ill. If a workman who is neither tired nor ill is making a poor job of what he is set to do, he is either not suited to the work or he has been inadequately trained.

The presence of rules like this in the Swindon book suggests that the railway management expected to rule by fear and knew no other way of preserving discipline. This is certainly the opinion of men who earned their living at Swindon Works before the First World War. They took the bullying and the pressurising for granted and did what they could to defend themselves against it, recognising that the ill-intentioned and unscrupulous foreman had no difficulty in interpreting the rules in a way that suited him. The rule book was, in effect, tailor-made to the foreman's requirements. With plenty of unemployment the other side of the perimeter wall, it was easier and safer to play to the foreman than to argue with him.

5
WOLVERTON AND STRATFORD

ALFRED Williams, some of whose descriptions of Swindon Works were quoted in the previous chapter, can hardly be called a typical workman. He was clearly out-of-place in the industrial environment and for this reason he probably reacted more strongly than most people to the conditions he documented in such a vivid and useful way. Most factory workers gradually become dulled to the work they have to do. They anaesthetise themselves to prevent themselves becoming unbearably hurt. Yet all workers must of necessity have some attitude towards their work, however rarely or successfully they put it into words. Nowadays, psychologists and sociologists go to great trouble to discover what people think about the way in which they have chosen or been compelled to earn a living, but for previous periods we can do little more than make deductions from such evidence as we have. These deductions may quite well be wrong, because there is always the danger of saying, in effect, 'This is how a modern factory-worker would have responded to the situation'. We do not make sufficient allowance for the remarkable ability people have to adapt themselves to circumstances and to remain reasonably contented, despite what their descendants would term gross exploitation and provocation. By today's standards, bloody revolution should have broken out several times a year at Swindon Works in the old days, but the important fact is that at Swindon as elsewhere men went quietly and regularly to their work. They did not strike, they did not chop the foreman into pieces and throw the bits into the canal, nor did they burn down the premises. They accepted their conditions, because they could see no alternative.

Conversations with men and women now in their eighties and nineties provide an invaluable insight into the effects which a harsh labour market had on a person's thoughts about jobs and discipline.

Mr Albert Healey, of Wolverton, was born in 1885 in a small village in North Buckinghamshire. His father and mother had eleven children. They had a small-holding which helped to eke out their income of 11s. a week. 'I remember,' he said,

my Mother and others to go off in the morning with a bucket and basket before the grass was dry to gather blackberries, they used to tramp miles in a day some times with a child or two hanging on all day, and when they got home they was tired out and what did they get for them three farthing a pound, and they would go to get mushrooms or send the children to get some if they could find any and they would sell them as well, when the harvest came they would go gleaning for a bit of corn to make a bit of flour, as I can tell you what with the corn out of the allotment, they use to have their own flour, as the Miller at that time of day would come and collect the corn to grind and bring back the flour, I have seen a bag of flour stand on a chair and a stick down the middle to help keep it from going musty, if they had not done those things at that time plenty would have starved and I can tell you the men at that time had to be very carefull or they would soon be out of work, and their was allways some one who wanted a place, and the children when they got older had to be like saints to get a place.[1]

Mr Healey left school when he was twelve, to work on a farm for half-a-crown a week. As he grew older, he asked for more money and got sacked on the spot. 'Work was scarce at that time. People wanted you to do a man's work for a boy's wages.' After a long succession of farm jobs—some good, some bad—he found himself out of work at the age of twenty-one, and decided to see what might be going at the L.N.W.R. Works at Wolverton.

The method of approach demanded a great deal of patience and pushing:

I did use to come every morning and stand out side as did others who was out of work. That is what you had to do at that time. Then the gate keeper came out and picked them out, but some had a letter from a Parson or someone well up to give to him so that could go to the Manager to see what they had to say about you. If it was a good report about you or from a chapel Parson you stood a chance of a job, as the Manager was a big chapel man and that made it a lot better for you if you got a letter from a chapel Parson, and that is what I did. I went and saw the one that married us and he gave me one to take to them and that was how I got in the Works, and not ashamed of it, as hundreds done the same and I wanted a job of work. That was January 1907 and I managed to stop their till September 1951.

I started at the wage of sixteen shillings a week and had to get there at six in the morning, breakfast at eight fifteen till nine o'clock, then one o'clock for dinner, back at two till five thirty, and that was the time you had to make Saturday till twelve. There was workmen from all round. Some came on foot from as far away as Calverton, Old Bradwell, Haversham, and all the villages round, some by train where they could get to the Station, and a lot from other places with a horse and four wheels, covered in in the winter and often in the summer there was about five or six of them from different villages, and the old steam tram from Stratford with little Billy as conductor it use to run up the middle of the road at some places and had points down the middle as well and a loop where they could change over engine from one end to the other, and they would hold up to hundred men top and bottom.

I did not like it at first shut up all day, and let out like a lot of sheep at meal time and going all different ways. Some of them could move faster than they did all day, but you get that in all places but some had to run back as well, but at that time you had to do as you was told and ask no questions, it is not like that today as if they do not like a job they give their notice and get another job, but at that time when I started their was not a lot of jobs outside so you done as you was told and did not want the sack.[2]

The Wolverton employees certainly had to watch their step, both inside and outside the Works. Mr Healey recalls that, soon after he began his employment there, 'if a man was caught after rabbits about the farms and was summoned for it, he got the sack from the Works. That was double punishment, one at the Police Court and the other the sack from work. Good old days, and you had to be very careful what you did at that time.'[3]

The innovation of regular holidays began in 1907:

It was ten days every holiday Easter, Whitsuntide, August, Christmas, ten days each time and short time in between at that. Railway workers to-day do not know what short time is. If they did they would not grumble so much. If they got the great wage of sixteen shillings a week, four long holidays without pay and short time in between, what a shock it would be for some of them to get that lot, and now some of them would work all the holiday that is paid for if they could draw the holiday pay as well. Talk about the good old times.[4]

Mr Lawrence began work at Wolverton in 1899. He was 23 at the time, and had served an apprenticeship as a carriage-builder elsewhere. He was originally engaged to make horse-drawn buses, a subsidiary business carried on by the Company within the railway works. Corruption was widespread, with the foremen as central figures. The system worked in this way. A gang of men signed a contract with a foreman to build a bus for a fixed price, which was always substantially less than the price allowed to the foreman by the Company. Each of the men had a copy of the agreement, but when the job had been completed they had to return their copies, so that the only record of the transaction remained with the foreman, as sub-contractor.

It was common for the foremen to run shops in Wolverton or Stony Stratford and to pay the gang partly in vouchers, exchangable only at their own shops. This was, of course, in total defiance of the Truck Act, but, in the words of Mr Healey, 'there was not a lot of jobs outside, so you done as you was told'. After the L.N.W.R. stopped making buses,

D

Mr Lawrence went on to vans and parcel carts and then to repairing passenger coaches.

No surviving rule book for Wolverton has come to light,[5] but the records for infringements, taken together with the reminiscences of elderly workers, suggest that the rules at Wolverton were very similar to those in force at Swindon. In February 1907, for instance, J. Allen, labourer, was discharged for 'insobriety'; while in March of the following year A. W. Barker, rough painter, was fined for 'losing time'. Drinking was forbidden anywhere in the works, and smoking everywhere except in the smithy. Eating was officially banned in the workshops, but went on none the less. Visits to the lavatory were strictly controlled. Lavatory-timing was carried out by a disabled man, who sat at a suitably placed desk 'with a big book', recording entrances and exits. Six minutes was the maximum time allowed.

At Wolverton, the foreman could fine and suspend, but only the management could dismiss. In Mr Lawrence's memory, men were most frequently suspended for being consistently late. The official timetable at the Works was:

                6.00–8.15
                8.15–9.00   Breakfast
                9.00–12.30
                12.30–1.30   Dinner
                1.30–5.30

Infringements of these rules must have been frequent, because a notice,[6] signed by C. A. Park, the Superintendent at Wolverton Works, and dated 7 July 1898, reads:

My attention has been called to the growing practice of the men leaving their work at meal times, before the whistle blows. This is against the rules and must be stopped. If my attention is again called to any man leaving his work before the proper time, he will hold himself liable to be dismissed.

A later notice, dated 8 November, also signed by Mr Park, attempts to deal with the problem from another angle, that of the time-checkers. If the men were in the habit of leaving early, the checkers had to co-operate by being there to record their departure. Mr Park therefore issued a stern warning to the clerks.

NOTICE: Clerks are not allowed in the passage for checking purposes before 3 minutes to the Whistle. Any one found there before that time, or who are late coming to the Office, will be severely dealt with.

In carriage-works it was customary for the men to provide most of their own tools.[7] These, when packed up together, filled a sizeable and heavy chest, so it was hardly surprising that they were not taken home each night. A notice posted up by Mr Park in 1883 is therefore somewhat surprising, at least in its ending:

The attention of Artisans, Workmen and others is called to the following Minute passed by the Directors at their meeting on 5th April 1883.
Resolved: That Artisans, Workmen and others in the service be informed that no allowance will in future be made by the Company towards Loss of Tools by Fire, and that the men must make their own arrangements to insure their Tools, as the Company cannot admit any liability in respect of Tools left on the Company's premises for the convenience of their owners.

A set of rules for the Stratford Works of the Great Eastern Railway survives in the British Transport Records.[8] It is dated July 1909 and falls into two parts, the first dealing with workshop discipline and the second with the procedure to be followed in the event of illness or disease.

WORKSHOP
RULES AND REGULATIONS

Rule I Terms of Engagement

No workman will be permanently employed in these works without a satisfactory certificate as to character from his last employers; he will be required to produce his certificate of birth and to sign a declaration that he has received a copy of these rules and binds himself to observe them.

Rule II Workmen not to Trade

Workmen are not allowed to trade either directly or indirectly for themselves or others, but must devote themselves exclusively to the Company's service.

Rule III Place of Entrance

Any workman entering or leaving the premises by any other way than through the gate at the Gate-keeper's offices, will render himself liable to dismissal.

Rule IV Checks

Every workman is required to receive at the check-office, each time he enters the works, a check bearing his number, and to deposit it, in the presence of the person in charge, each time he leaves. No workman shall, under any circumstances whatever, receive or deposit another workman's check. Any workman neglecting to take his check on entering the works, or to deposit it on leaving, will lose the time such checks should cover. Any man losing or defacing his check will have to pay sixpence for another.

Rule V Working Hours

The week shall consist of 54 hours, commencing at 6 a.m. on Saturday, and shall be divided as under:

Saturday	6.00 a.m. to 8.15 a.m. 9.00 a.m. to 12 noon	} paid for as 5¼ hours
Monday		
Tuesday	6.00 a.m. to 8.15 a.m.	
Wednesday	9.00 a.m. to 1.00 p.m.	} paid as for 9¾ hours per day
Thursday	2.00 p.m. to 5.30 p.m.	
Friday		

The bell for entering shall be rung first at 5.40 a.m. and again at 5.55 a.m., five minutes before 9.00 a.m., and five minutes before 2 p.m., and each man must be at his place in the shop, ready to commence his work, at six o'clock, nine o'clock and two o'clock. The bell for leaving the works shall be rung at 8.15 a.m. for breakfast, 1.00 p.m. for dinner, and at 5.30 p.m., except on Saturday, when it shall be rung at 12 noon. No man must leave his work till the bell has rung.

Men employed more than these working hours shall be paid time and a quarter for the first two hours, and time and a half afterwards.

The full ordinary time for the day must be made before overtime is reckoned.

Sunday, Good Friday and Christmas Day, will be paid for at the rate of time and a half, but men working regularly or alternately during the night, or on Sunday, will be paid at the ordinary rates.

N.B. – this rule does not apply to forgemen or other men working at the steam hammers, examiners, carriage cleaners, watchmen, stationary enginemen and firemen, and running shed staff (except mechanics and assistants), who will continue to work such hours and be paid as may be specially agreed.

Except where otherwise announced the payment of wages will take place on Fridays for the week ending the Friday previous.

Rule VI Losing Time

Any workman absenting himself from works without permission will render himself liable to dismissal. When unavoidably absent he must notify his Foreman, and state the cause.

Rule VII Absence from Pay Table

Workmen unable to attend at the pay table must use the printed form, countersigned by the Foreman, authorizing some one to receive their money.

Rule VIII Attention to Duties

(1) Workmen are cautioned against playing or idling during working hours, or unless with special permission, washing before the bell rings. Workmen are forbidden, in any circumstances, to wash their hands in oil. (2) No workman is allowed to go into a shop in which he is not usually employed, except by order of his foreman. (3) Any workman quarrelling, using improper language, or otherwise misconducting himself, or not cheerfully and carefully carrying out instructions, will render himself liable to dismissal.

Rule IX Personal Tools

Every workman must provide himself with such personal tools as are usual in his trade. Tool chests will be examined by the Foreman before they are allowed to be taken out of the Works.

Rule X Shop Tools

Every workman will be required to see that each of his shop tools bears the initials of the Company, and any workman borrowing tools from another must be careful to return them immediately they are done with. A list of each workman's tools must be kept. When any workman requires a new tool he must apply to his Foreman, who will supply it if necessary. All new tools must be obtained at the shop stores on a Foreman's request, and the old tools given up at the same time.

Rule XI General Shop Tools

Any workman using taps, dies, reamers, gauges or templates must see that when done with they are immediately returned in good condition to the person appointed to take charge of them. If attention is not called to any defects or damage at the time they are taken out of the store, it will be considered proof that they were then in good order, and if any of them be lost or damaged, the man by whom they were taken out will be held responsible. Private tools are not allowed to be made in the shops under penalty of instant dismissal.

Rule XII Locks

A lock and key will be supplied in the first instance to each workman, if any of them be lost or damaged, the man by whom they were taken out will be held responsible. Private tools are not allowed to be made in the shops under penalty of instant dismissal.

Rule XIII Caution as to Use of Material

Any workman making use of material which is imperfect or unfit for the intended purpose, or putting upon the scrap heap material which is otherwise ideal, or carelessly wasting material in any way, will be dealt with as the case may deserve.

Rule XIV Old Material not to be taken away

No material, however old or apparently worthless, must in any circumstances be taken off the premises.

Rule XV Use of Soft Soap, &c

For turning and machinery work soft soap and water only are to be used, except in cases where oil is specially allowed by the Foreman.

Great care must be taken that no dirty or greasy waste is left lying about or allowed to accumulate; and such material must be placed in the bin appointed. No clean sponge cloths will be issued without the old ones being returned. Sponge cloths must not be cut up or mutilated.

Rule XVI Use of Templates and Drawings

Any workman making articles of wrong dimensions, or finishing work in an inferior or unworkmanlike manner, will be dealt with as the case may deserve. In no case must drawings or templates be altered without the sanction of the Works Manager.

Rule XVII Time keeping

It is the duty of the Time-Keeper to appropriate the time made by the workmen, as well as to take an account of it; workmen are therefore required to give him correct and sufficient information. Any workman giving incorrect or insufficient information will render himself liable to dismissal.

Rule XVIII Precautions against Fire

Every workman using a fire is required to see that it is left safe at meal hours, and put out when he is leaving work for the day; when blast is used it must be shut off on each occasion.

Great care must be taken by all workmen to avoid any and every possible risk of fire.

Rule XIX Extinguishing Lights

Every workman must turn off the gas and as far as possible put out any other lights he has been using, before going to meals or leaving off work.

Rule XX Closing of Shops

At meal hours every man, except those specially authorised to remain, must leave the works, which will be closed until five minutes before the bell commences to ring. The dining rooms are to be considered as outside the works.

Rule XXI Intoxicating Liquors Prohibited

Any person bringing intoxicating liquors into the works will be dealt with as the case may deserve.

Rule XXII Introduction of Strangers

Any workman bringing a stranger on to the premises without the sanction of the Foreman will render himself liable to dismissal.

Rule XXIII Smoking Prohibited

Smoking is strictly prohibited either in or about the workshops or Company's premises, and any workman found smoking will be liable to dismissal.

Rule XXIV Damage to Machines

Any workman injuring a machine or other article through carelessness or neglect, or leaving anything foul of the 18-inch tramway, will be dealt with as the case may deserve.

Rule XXV Leaving the Works

No workman will be allowed to pass out of the works during working hours without a printed pass signed by his Foreman, nor will any one be allowed at any time to take out of the works any tool or material, unless specified by his Foreman upon a pass, and the number of pieces stated. All passes must be left with the Gatekeeper, who is required to take an account of material of any kind passing from the works through his gate.

Rule XXVI Accidents

Any workman meeting with an accident must at once report the occurrence to his Foreman.

Rule XXVII Infectious Diseases

The following are the conditions regulating the attendance at work of workmen residing at a house where a case of Small Pox, Cholera, Diphtheria, Scarlet Fever or Scarlatina, or Typhus Fever breaks out.

A workman living at home with his family will not be allowed to resume work until he can produce a certificate (Form A) that it is perfectly safe, so far as regards his fellow workmen, for him to do so, and also a certificate from the Infectious Diseases Fund or the Local Authorities (Form B) that his house has been thoroughly and efficiently disinfected. In the case of Small Pox, a workman will not be allowed to resume work until 14 days after the date of Certificate "B".

A workman residing in lodgings, and who removes to other lodgings immediately the existence of infectious disease is made known, will be allowed to attend his work on production of the Medical Certificate (Form A), provided he gives a written guarantee (Form C) that he will not return to, nor visit, nor hold any communication with his original lodgings, nor associate with any of the occupants thereof until such time as such lodgings have been certified to be thoroughly and efficiently disinfected.

But a workman, whether living at home with his family or in lodgings will be allowed to attend work on production of a Medical Certificate (Form D), to the satisfaction of the head of his Department, that the case has been thoroughly and efficiently isolated, and that it is perfectly safe, so far as his fellow workmen are concerned, for him to return to work, such Certificate to be renewed weekly until the production of a Certificate (Form B) that the house has been thoroughly and efficiently disinfected.

Workmen compelled to absent themselves from work under these Regulations will be allowed half wages by the Company while so absent, provided they are Members of an Infectious Diseases Fund recognised by the Company. The Company will not make any allowance to men who may themselves be laid up with any of the Scheduled diseases, such cases being met by the ordinary Provident and Friendly Societies.

Form A

I hereby certify that it is perfectly safe, so far as his fellow workmen and the public are concerned, for ...., at whose residence there has been a case of ...., to attend his work on the Great Eastern Railway.

Form B

I hereby certify that ...., the house at which ...., resides, and at which there has been a case of ...., has been thoroughly and efficiently disinfected.

Form C

I, ..., hereby state that a case of .... having broken out at .... where I lodge, I have with the sanction of Dr. .... immediately removed to ...., and I promise not to return to, nor visit, not hold any communication with my original lodgings, nor associate with any of the occupants thereof until such time as the house in question has been certified by the Local Authorities or the Infectious Diseases Fund to have been thoroughly and efficiently disinfected.

Form D

I hereby certify that the case of ...., at ...., where .... resides, has been thoroughly and efficiently isolated from the outset of the disease, and that it is perfectly safe, so far as his fellow workmen and the public are concerned, for .... to attend his work on the Great Eastern Railway.

Rule XXVIII Passes and Privilege Tickets

Any workman travelling with a pass, and neglecting to give up the same to the Station Master or Ticket Collector at the end of each journey or when otherwise required, will be dealt with as the case may deserve.

Misuse of a pass or privilege ticket will render the offender liable to dismissal.

Rule XXIX Leaving the Company's Service

A Workman leaving the service of the Company will forfeit any wages in hand unless he has given a Week's notice. He must deliver to his Foreman the key of his drawer or tool chest, and satisfactorily account for the tools charged against him.

S. D. Holden
Locomotive Superintendent

Crewe Works were established in 1843, as the locomotive works of the Grand Junction Railway Company. They were built to take the place of Edge Hill Shops. The work was carried out under the supervision of Francis Trevithick, who was appointed as the first Locomotive Superintendent. At that time, the Works covered 2½ acres and 161 men were employed there. In 1846 Crewe became the Works of the London and North-Western Railway.

In 1862 the locomotive side of Wolverton Works of the old London and Birmingham Railway was closed and the construction and maintenance of all locomotives for the L.N.W.R. was transferred to Crewe, under the control of John Ramsbottom, who was appointed Locomotive Superintendent.

In 1936 a booklet[1] was issued by the L.M.S. Railway to celebrate the centenary of the birth of F. E. Webb who, more than anyone else, had been responsible for the development of the Works at Crewe. Webb followed two great locomotive pioneers and epitomises the old railway paternalism in the kind of one-industry town where the life of every family was in some way bound up with the railway works. 'The late Mr Webb,' says the booklet,

was born within a few miles of Crewe on May 21st, 1836, and spent practically all his life in the service of the London and North Western Railway. He rose from an apprentice to the position of Chief Mechanical Engineer in the Company, and for many years had charge of the great locomotive works at Crewe which were regarded as the leading railway locomotive works which constituted a natural training ground for those who aspired to high positions in the mechanical engineering departments of railways, or in the locomotive industry, in this country and in other parts of the world. The great reputation held by Crewe Works—where at one

period during Mr Webb's sojourn, nearly 10,000 men were employed—
in the annals of British Locomotive History, resulted largely from the
efforts of a succession of notable Locomotive Superintendents and Chief
Mechanical Engineers. Mr Webb succeeded such great locomotive engineers as F. Trevithick and John Ramsbottom. The influence exerted by Mr
Webb on the trend of locomotive evolution, both in this country and
abroad, helped to realise this fact.

Mr Webb's connection with Crewe extended over half a century with an
interval of five years spent in other work. He was the second son of the
Rector of Tixall in Staffordshire, where he was born. His brother became
Vicar of St Paul's Church at Crewe. During the time Mr. F. W. Webb was
at Crewe he supervised the building of over 4,000 locomotives, turning
them out at the rate of 110 to 146 a year. He entered Crew Works in 1851—
eight years after they were established—as a pupil of the late Mr Trevithick, who was the first locomotive superintendent and the son of Richard
Trevithick . . . Mr F. W. Webb was appointed chief draughtsman in 1859,
and Works Manager about two years later, a position which he held for five
years, resigning it to become manager of the Bolton Iron and Steel Co.
Five years later, however, he returned to Crewe and succeeded Mr John
Ramsbottom as mechanical engineer and locomotive superintendent of the
L. and N. W. Railway Company, a position which he held until his retire-
ment over thirty years later.

During that period Crewe grew from a place of 18,000 inhabitants to a
town with a population of over 40,000, and practically every family depended for its livelihood upon the Works which were then considered to be the
largest locomotive engine works in the world. The Railway Company
built thousands of cottages for their workpeople; they built seven schools
for the children, and also Christ Church which they endowed.

Mr Webb was the head of a huge family. His staff in the later years of
his service numbered well over 10,000. He encouraged the sons of all
employees to enter the Works. Boys were destined for Crewe Works almost
immediately after their birth. It was only natural with such great interests
in the town, that Mr Webb should identify himself with the government
of the Borough. He was one of the first members of the Town Council, and
was elected Mayor of the Borough on two occasions. He was also made
a Freeman of the Borough. It was entirely through Mr Webb's influence
that the beautiful Park was presented to the town; it was due to him that
the Cottage Hospital was built; it was he, too, who created the Mechanics'
Institution, and he was also responsible for the formation of the Crewe
Volunteer Engineer Corps, which during the South African War sent out
400 skilled men to be attached to the Royal Engineers. These men did
splendid work in maintaining the railways in Africa.

Webb died in 1906. He made large local bequests, some of which went to
found the Webb Orphanage. In a very real sense he was Crewe. He had
his finger on everything of significance that went on in the town and he
ran the Works in a strongly autocratic way.[2]

Mr Leslie Cooper began work under Webb in 1902, when he was
fourteen. He earned 16s. a week when he started in the plate mill, which
was nearly as much as an adult labourer got. His father was paid only
18s. a week, out of which he rented a three-bedroomed Company house
for 3s. 6d. and somehow supported a family. From the plate shop

Cooper moved first to the tyre mill, then to the drop hammers, and afterwards to the melting furnaces, working both day and night shifts, usually a fortnight on days and a fortnight on nights. By the time he was eighteen he was earning 35s. 7d. a week.

Conditions of employment were very strict. No smoking was allowed. Suspension was the usual penalty, but Mr Cooper recalls that on one occasion a man was dismissed on the spot for knocking out an unlit pipe against a door-post.[3] Employees were not allowed to wash their hands, under pain of instant dismissal. Two visits to the lavatory in one day could mean suspension. Men had to hand in their work-check to a specially posted attendant when they went into the lavatory and collect it when they came out. The attendant recorded the time and frequency of visits and if either was held to be excessive the offender had to write a letter of explanation to the manager.[4]

Time-keeping could hardly have been more tightly controlled if every man had been paid a pound a minute. For those not engaged on regular shift work, the weekly total, until 1918, was 54 hours, 9¾ hours a day from Monday to Friday and 5¼ on Saturdays.

Situated throughout the Works, in the vicinity of the entrances to the workshops, were small cabins or check boxes. These cabins were about four feet in width and eight to ten feet in length, with a door and a small window on each long side. As the men filed by one of the windows they called out their allotted number and a check-lad handed them a metal check bearing that number. When they left off work at the end of a shift they threw in the check at their particular box window. These checks were collected by the check-lads for sorting into sets of checks, one for mornings and one for afternoons, and in addition, a separate set of pay checks, made of brass. The brass checks were handed out each Friday at 2 p.m., instead of the ordinary metal check, and as the men filed by their respective window at the end of this shift they received a pay tin for the brass check. The money was taken out of the tin by the man, and if correct, the empty tin was placed in a hamper which was situated outside the cabin.

In addition to the checks, a small hard-backed canvas book was issued to each man, for recording details of charges and hours covering his work. These 'time books' were issued as the men filed into work past the check box window at 9 a.m. each Tuesday.

The check-lads were under the supervision of a Time-keeper who generally looked after one or two boxes. The Time-keeper was responsible for recording absentees and those booking on late. A man was allowed to draw his check, or time book, up to 15 minutes following the beginning of a shift, i.e. 6.15 a.m., 9.15 a.m., and 2.15 p.m. If a man failed to draw his check before these times he had to lose the time up to the commencement of the next shift. The windows in the check boxes were of the sash window type and could be operated up and down by a cord controlled by the check-lad, who, smartly at 6 a.m., 9 a.m., and 2 p.m., dropped the window and prevented any more checks being issued. After a brief pause the window would be lifted and the issue of checks would be made to the late comers up to fifteen minutes following the commencement of the shift.

After each 'booking-on' period the Time-keeper recorded the checks or time books which had not been given out for entry into the check book at the Time Office. The same information was also given a Shop Clerk for the Shop's Absentee Record. Symbols were used to record absentee time in the following manner:—

⌒ absent 6 a.m. to 8.15 a.m.	↑↘ absent 9 a.m. to 9.15 a.m.
↑ absent 6 a.m. to 6.15 a.m.	╱ absent 2 p.m. to 5.30 p.m.
↘ absent 9 a.m. to 1.00 p.m.	╱↑ absent 2 p.m. to 2.15 p.m.

A full day's absence would be recorded as ◊ or combinations to represent any of the items shown.

All these booking-on activities and the time recordings were controlled from three Time Offices—one for the Old Works (East end), one for the Deviation (middle area of the Works) and one for the West end (or Steel Works). From these offices Time-keepers went out to cover the time-booking in all the workshops. In the Time Offices all details were assembled and checked and pay bills made out for wages to be paid.

The Time-keepers went into their allotted areas and entered in the man's time book details of work done, together with particulars of the orders concerned. Black ink was used to denote daywork (i.e. time which was not to include any piecework balance) and red ink for the piecework items. A novel feature about the booking of time in the shops was the arrangement the Time-keeper had for carrying his ink around. For this purpose he had two small glass bottles fixed in a leather holder which was buttoned on his jacket, and a double ended pen, with a nib at one end for black ink and at the other end a nib for red ink. There were no corks or stoppers to the bottles, but the necks were so made as to prevent any spilling of ink.

The wages details were made up to Thursday night of each week and payment was always a week in hand. The wages drawn one week would represent the earnings up to Thursday evening of the previous week. Consequently, newcomers had to work for two weeks before they received any wages.[5]

Until well into the 1930's there was little alternative employment in the Crewe area, except in agriculture. Mr Cooper himself used to get up at four in the morning and had an hour's walk to get to the Works by six. He recalls that some men walked for more than two hours each way.

Foremen at Crewe tended to run in families. Most of them lived in De La Mare Street, which was where the managers lived too. They were difficult to recruit,[6] at least in the 'twenties and afterwards, because they earned less than some of the men on the shop floor. Mr R. A. Riddles, who was a premium apprentice at Crewe, remembers the Manager coming round and asking 'Who wants a bowler hat?' Few people did, and consequently the foremen were 'not all that brilliant'.

On the other hand, they enjoyed much greater security of employment than the men they supervised[7] and they had full control over their men. Disciplinary powers began to be taken from them in the early 1930's. Previously, the foreman simply dismissed or suspended a man. The new system was for the foreman to issue Form 1, which meant 'You're going to be suspended, but you can appeal'. The appeal was Company head-quarters at Euston and eventually the man in question appeared before a local Committee with his union representative to advise him.

At Crewe, as at most of the other railway works, the chances of be-coming apprenticed to a skilled trade were very small unless one's father was already employed by the Company. Given the family link, it was necessary to pass Grade 7 in an elementary school and to make a satis-factory showing at an oral examination. There was then usually a wait of about six months, after which the new apprentice started off as a kind of engineering office-boy, taking round oil and cotton-waste to the dif-ferent departments. No organised instruction was given, apart from a restricted system of day-release, known as 'Friday afternoon school'. The apprentice had to pick up his skills as best he could. The Time-Office was responsible for moving the apprentices around the Works, to make sure they got a variety of experience. The Time-Office was, in fact, the precursor of the Establishment Department.

All the railway companies had premium apprentices, who paid as much as £200 for the privilege. In the earlier part of this century the London and North Western took on sixty a year. They received no particular privileges as apprentices, although the fact that most of them had had a better education before beginning their apprenticeship—a number were public-schoolboys—usually meant that they went much further in their later careers. There was some tendency for the premium apprentices to regard themselves as belonging to a class apart. During the 1911 strike, for instance, the premium apprentices helped to keep the railways running and were very unpopular in the Works afterwards.

Yet many of the men who came to hold leading positions on the rail-ways served their time as premium apprentices, and their early training in the workshop, together with the fact that they usually lodged with railwaymen's families, gave them a close acquaintanceship with the way ordinary working men lived. R. A. Riddles, who carried through much of the reorganisation at both Crewe and Derby Works during the 1920's and later became Member for Engineering at the British Railways Board, noted that the man who gave him lodgings as an apprentice earned only 32s. a week, but had nevertheless contrived to buy both his own house and two others in the town. He also saw that the men were exhausted after working a twelve-hour day and that 'their hobbies were the hobbies of exhausted men—pigeons, canary-breeding, fishing'.[8]

There was no system of sickness pay apart from what the men could get from their clubs, but, as Riddles remembers it, there was very little absence from work because of sickness. During the whole of his apprenticeship he never saw a Factory Inspector in the Works. There were strict rules about using machinery, especially grindstones, and about straying into other departments.[9] Accidents were investigated by the Time Office Clerk and the foreman of the shop. If an accident could be shown to be the victim's own fault, either through carelessness or through being in a part of the Works which was forbidden to him, no compensation was payable. Otherwise, compensation came from a fund built up by a contribution of 1s. a week deducted from each man's wages.

There is a difference of opinion as to whether there was ever a rule book at Crewe Works. Mr C. A. Townsend, now in retirement, entered his employment there during the First World War, under the Chief Engineer, Bohen Cook. He remembered[10] what he called 'a small rule book'. It listed the conditions of service, gave the penalties for misconduct, such as dismissal for drunkenness at work, and provided information about the Hospital Fund. During his early years' service with the Company, there were hand-written notices at each entrance to the Works, and what he described as 'printed rules posted at each gate in a glass frame'. These were almost certainly the summaries of the Factories Act, not Company Rules.

Mr R. A. Riddles, on the other hand, who began work at Crewe rather earlier than Mr Townsend, has no recollection of seeing or hearing about any rule book, and doubts if the habit existed at Wolverton either. He has an interesting theory as to why the Great Western and North Eastern Railways went in for rule books at their Works and why the L.N.W.R. did not. The Great Western and the North Eastern Works, it appears, were controlled by the operating side, and 'the operators always worked to rule'. On the L.N.W.R., however, the Works at Crewe and Derby were controlled by the Chief Mechanical Engineer, who was a powerful, autonomous figure, admitting no connexion whatever with the operating side of his own railway. This independence went so far that the Works shunting engines were always driven by men on the payroll of the Chief Mechanical Engineer.

It is possible to suggest that the L.N.W.R. allowed its Chief Mechanical Engineers too much independence. During the early part of the present century and into the 'twenties the man in charge at Crewe was Beams, whom Riddles has described as 'a very autocratic man'. Beams had always worked at Crewe and had had the opportunity of watching the great Webb in action. At the outbreak of war in 1914 he was Captain Beams, of the Territorials. Ambitious men in Crewe came to realise that it was a great advantage to join the Territorials. In Riddles' words, 'You met the bosses there'. Elsewhere, as under Sir Josiah Stamp, wise men discovered a close sympathy with the Methodists.

In 1923, the L.N.W.R. was absorbed into the new L.M.S. group. Riddles was given responsibility for the Progress Office, and sent for a spell to Horwich to look at the methods in use there. He found them 'very far ahead'. 'They had micrometers and we had calipers.' There were, in his opinion, three main reasons for the superiority of Horwich over Crewe—the works was 'much younger'; Walkland, the machine-shop foreman, was an exceptionally able man; and the foremen at Horwich had more authority than at Crewe.

Horwich had developed the extremely sensible system of examining engines first before they were sent for overhaul. At Crewe, on the other hand—as at Horwich before the War—the work was very wastefully organised. To make sure the maximum number of engines was available during the busy summer months, engines came to Crewe for overhaul before they had done the required number of miles. Beams refused to install the Horwich system, despite Riddles' attempts to persuade him of its great advantage. The Chief Mechanical Engineer's comment was a typical one, '£3,000 a year and we get nothing for it'. This degree of conservatism was not helpful to either the railways or their workshops during the 'twenties and 'thirties. From being rightly respected as pioneers in engineering during the nineteenth century, they became a by-word for backward methods and inefficiency during the twentieth. Management, as well as worker, had their rule books and not infrequently worked to them.

Crewe, at any rate, was very much an engineer's Works. In the first century of its life it was ruled over by only five men: Trevithick, Ramsbottom, Webb, Beams and Stanier—three of them outstanding engineers and all men of a strongly autocratic turn of mind. The first three appear to have left remarkably few of their battle-orders behind them. Their written notices and rules were either rarely issued or rapidly destroyed once their original purpose had been served.

Most of the surviving rules and orders from the nineteenth century are of this type:

NOTICE
On and after Monday, 30 October, the first Whistle will be blown at 5.30 a.m. instead of 5.40.
The second whistle will remain as at present.
Engine Works
Crewe, 27 October 1871

Free tickets were evidently causing problems, although they can hardly be described as serious:

NOTICE

My attention having been recently called by the Secretary to two
cases of Company's servants using Orders for Free Tickets as Free
Passes, instead of changing them at the Booking Offices for Tickets
(one for the outward and the other for the return journey) NOTICE is
hereby given that in all similar instances in future I shall leave the
Authorities at Euston to deal with them in the usual way as they
would do in the case of ordinary Passengers.

Engine Works
Crewe, 26 October 1871

One curious type of offence is pilloried in another notice of that year:

NOTICE TO WORKMEN

The great increase in the number of applications made by Workmen
for permission to show their Friends through these Works is causing
serious inconvenience in the shops, and Workmen are hereby cautioned
not to make such frequent applications in future, or it may be found
necessary to withdraw the privilege altogether, except at holiday
times (and then only when the Works are open).

Engine Works, Crewe
16th November 1871

The Orders covered all aspects of the men's lives. Here is one about a
problem of hygiene:

As small-pox is now prevalent in the town of Crewe, it is of the
utmost importance that all dwelling houses should be kept as clean as
possible.

Workmen are recommended to limewash their premises and any of
the Company's tenants may obtain whitewash for this purpose on application to the office of the Estate Department, Crewe.

Engine Works,
Crewe. 18th March 1872

The first workshop at Derby was built in 1840, when a joint passenger
station for three companies—the Midland Counties, the North Midland
and the Birmingham and Derby Junction—was completed. In 1844 the
three companies amalgamated, forming the Midland Railway Company,
with head office and centre of operations at Derby. At that time the combined Locomotive and Carriage and Wagon Works occupied a total area
of $8\frac{1}{2}$ acres, with buildings and workshops covering $2\frac{1}{2}$ acres, much the
same as at Crewe.

Mr Harry Pearce[11] began work in the body shop at Derby in 1896, as a
carriage-builder. He was the son of a railwayman and he was taken on by
the foreman, who recommended to the Superintendent of the Works

that he should be employed as an apprentice and taught the trade.[12] He signed no indentures and was given no formal contract of service.

For the whole of Mr Pearce's working life, Derby had a good variety of employment to offer. A man was not dependent on the railway there, as he was at Crewe and Swindon,[13] although in the 1890's, when Mr Pearce began his apprenticeship, a job at the railway works was much sought after. A man who belonged there could—and did—say he had, on the whole, the best employer in the town. Derby's good fortune in not having all its eggs in one basket became apparent during the slump of the 1920's and 1930's, when the local unemployment figures were the lowest in the country.

It is quite possible that the presence of alternative employers in the district prevented the railway management at Derby from imposing as severe a discipline on their employees as was found elsewhere. The system of fines, for instance, never existed at Derby. The foremen had powers to suspend[14] or reprimand a man, and often did. They could also recommend dismissal for insubordination and bad work, and it was rare for the Company to disregard their advice. The Derby foremen never formed a clan, however, as they did in the one-industry railway towns. The grandfather-to-father-to-son chain was hardly ever found among the foremen there. Yet, if the Derby foremen were not a class, they were certainly a caste. Before about 1905 they never mixed with the men, either socially or at meal-times; the management would have strongly disapproved of such an excess of democracy. Even much later, in the 1940's, the foremen had a separate club of their own.

Probably because there were no fines at Derby, there was no rule book or other form of service-contract for a man to be given to sign. A copy of the Truck Act was, nevertheless, hung up in every shop in the Works. A new recruit, Mr Pearce remembers, picked up the rules of the place as he went along. There were notice-boards on which, for many years, only the Company's rules might be put. In the late 'twenties, however, the Company allowed Trade Union matters to be publicised there too. The Union never demanded that the men in the Works should be issued with any forms of rules and regulations or formal contract of employment.

The normal industrial discipline of the time applied at Derby during most of the period of Mr Pearce's employment there. Alcohol was forbidden in the Works, even to the foundrymen, for whom the great heat made beer almost a necessity. No smoking was officially allowed until 1936, although during the preceding twenty years the lavatories had a secondary function as a more or less tolerated cigarette-area.

E

No time was allowed for clearing-up operations, but they were expected to be done. The Company supplied some tools—files, spanners, hammers—but, in the carriage-works at least, each workman owned most of his tools and was responsible for their safety. A man needed a special pass in order to take even his own tools out of the Works.

The foremen at Derby enjoyed one form of power which would be unthinkable nowadays. They decided the rate at which a man was to be paid. Consequently rates varied a good deal, even for the same job. What a man got above the minimum rate depended on how well the foreman liked him. Anyone who had got on the wrong side of the foreman was almost obliged to move if he wanted more money.

At the end of his apprenticeship, Mr Pearce, like most of his fellow-apprentices, left the Company and moved round the country, looking all the time for better conditions and better pay, and taking his large and immensely heavy box of tools with him wherever he went. In 1908 he came back to Derby after finding work elsewhere increasingly hard to get. He was able to return to his old job only as a result of his father's influence with the foremen. The elder Mr Pearce did painting and paper-hanging in the foremen's houses and in this way had got to know a number of them well. In this particular instance, employment was difficult to find because Mr Pearce's trade was a specialised one. Had he been a skilled engineer instead of a skilled coach-builder, Derby, like the rest of the country, would have had more to offer him, and currying favour with the foremen would not have been so necessary.

DURING the later 1920's and the 1930's the growing power of the Trade Unions, and the gradual impact of the new idea that workers should be persuaded rather than threatened, produced throughout industry the beginnings of fundamental changes in the rules which employees were required to observe. While unemployment continued, these changes were slow to develop, but the totally different labour conditions brought about by the 1939–45 war accelerated the disappearance of the old world of master and man in which fear of being out of work subdued the will to protest against exploitation and injustice. Once politicians felt obliged to maintain something close to full employment, the traditional industrial discipline was dead.

It is interesting in this connexion to compare the 1904 Swindon rules, reproduced above (p. 35), with the revised version introduced in 1929. Apart from the final sentence relating to gas-makers and furnacemen, Section 2, which dealt with hours of work, was completely rewritten, as follows:

The standard hours agreed for railways will be worked. Overtime will be reckoned after the standard hours have been worked, and will be valued at the rate of time and a quarter for the first two hours, and time and a half afterwards. This clause applies only to men who have worked the full number of hours the works are open during the week except in the case of men off duty sick, or who have received bona fide leave, when they will not be expected to make good the time lost.

Men not regularly employed on Sundays will be paid double time for Sunday duty, i.e. between 12.0 midnight Saturday and 12.0 midnight Sunday. This rate also applies to Christmas Day and Good Friday.

This new Section embodies several important concessions to the men. The rate for Sunday overtime was raised from time-and-a-half to double-time, while Christmas Day and Good Friday were treated in the same way as Sundays. By 1929 the standard working week had been reduced from 54 to 48 hours, so that overtime became payable a good deal sooner. The normal week still had to be worked before a man was entitled to overtime—plotting this on a daily, rather than a weekly basis was still a long time ahead—but a new principle was introduced whereby time lost through illness no longer had to be made up before overtime could be claimed. When one considers the poor state of the national economy at that time, changes of this order marked a major triumph of good sense and Union bargaining power.

In 1904 it had been a condition of service that a man should belong to the Great Western's Sick and Medical Fund. A quarter of a century later, however, basic medical care was being provided by the State and so Section 3 no longer had the same point as previously and was omitted altogether.

The old agreement laid down that an engagement could be terminated by either party giving nine hours' notice. In 1929 this was changed to the more civilised period of seven working days. A further improvement is to be found in the new Section 5, by which a man could now be away from work for half a day, instead of a quarter of a day, without having to notify his foreman when he returned.

The system of fines, which had been in force for nearly a century, was swept away altogether. This was no more than an official recognition of the fact that the power to levy fines had been little used for some years. So, instead of a workman being liable to a fine of 6d. for not dealing properly with his job sheet, he 'will be reprimanded'. This reprimand came, of course, from the foreman, who was now expected to control without the help of fines all such misdemeanours as oiling machines without permission, smoking in the Works, wandering into forbidden parts of the premises and turning out sub-standard work.

Curiously, Section 37, which prohibited a man from trading while in the Company's service, was now removed altogether. The reason for this is not clear. It may well have been difficult to enforce at any time. What point was there, for instance, in stopping someone from selling eggs or vegetables to a colleague, or from dealing in a second-hand pram or piano? But the worsening of the country's economic position may have made it inevitable that men would look for second-hand bargains rather than buy goods new, and the factory or workshop was a perfectly natural and sensible market-place for such transactions.

The 1929 revision of the Great Western *Rules and Regulations* for workshop staff continued in force until the railways were nationalised in 1954. Long before that time, however, the Company anticipated the present policy of the British Railways Board and began a system of formal reminders to men employed in the workshops that they were railwaymen first and boiler-makers or upholsterers second. A poster[1] of 1933 shows how this was done:

Great Western Railway
Rules for observance by workshop staff
(extracted from the Book of Rules, dated 1st January 1933)

1. All employees must reside at whatever places may be appointed, attend at such hours as may be required, pay prompt obedience to persons placed in authority over them, conform to all the Rules and Regulations of the Company, and apart from the Company's business must not engage in trade.

Every employee must assist in carrying out the Rules and Regulations, and must immediately report to his superior officer any infringement thereof, or any occurrence which may come under his notice affecting safe and proper working.

The name and address of each employee must be recorded at the station to which he is attached, and any change of address must be at once notified.

Employees may, from time to time, be required to undergo medical, eyesight, practical or educational examinations in accordance with the regulations in force.

An employee must not leave the service of the Company without giving the notice required by the terms of his employment.

When an employee leaves the service he must immediately deliver up his uniform and all other articles belonging to the Company. Any pay due to any employee leaving the service will not be paid until the uniform and all other articles the property of the Company, supplied to him, shall have been delivered up or satisfactorily accounted for. If any article be not delivered up, be missing, or be damaged by improper use, the value of such article, or the cost of repair of any damage, shall be a debt due from the employee to the Company, and may (subject to the provisions of the Truck Acts) be deduced from any pay then due, or, if such pay be found insufficient to meet the claim, will become a debt recoverable at law.

2. Employees must, if required, make good any article provided by the Company when damaged by improper use on their part.

3. Employees must not:

    (i) absent themselves from or exchange duty, or alter appointed hours of attendance, without permission from their superior officers. In case of illness, the employee concerned must immediately advise his superior officer and furnish a medical certificate in accordance with the regulations.

(ii) appropriate to their own use any property of the Company.
(iii) waste or wantonly destroy stationery, stores or any other property of the Company.
(iv) consume intoxicating liquor whilst on duty.
4. The Company may at any time
  (i)   dismiss without notice; or
  (ii) suspend from duty, and, after enquiry, dismiss without notice, or
  (iii) suspend from duty as a disciplinary measure an employee of the Company for any one or more of the following offences, viz.
  (a) Drunkenness
  (b) Disobedience of orders
  (c) Misconduct or negligence
  (d) Absence from duty without leave

An employee so dismissed forfeits any right to notice and also any right to wages for any period subsequent to the completed week preceding his dismissal, or preceding his suspension from duty prior to dismissal as the case may be.

An employee suspended from duty pending enquiry and not exonerated, if not dismissed, may as part of the punishment awarded be deprived of any or all of the wages accruing to him in respect of the period subsequent to the completed week preceding his suspension and in respect of the period of his suspension as to the Company may seem just and reasonable.

An employee suspended from duty as a disciplinary measure forfeits any right to wages for the period subsequent to the completed week preceding his suspension, and for the period of his suspension.
5. The Company reserve the right to deduct from the pay of an employee, who is a tenant of the Company, any sums due for rent.
11. No employee shall expose himself to danger, and he must prevent as far as possible such exposure on the part of other employees, and spare no opportunity of warning those who neglect to take proper care.

Reckless exposure of himself or others to danger, on the part of any employee, is an offence against the Company's regulations and will be punished accordingly.
15. Employees are expressly prohibited from walking upon the line or crossing the rails (except at a public level crossing) unless they are required to do so in the execution of their duty or are proceeding to and from their work by a route permitted by the Company. Any employee walking upon the line or crossing the rails, except as aforesaid, will be acting outside his employment.

This is hardly a revolutionary document and it does no more than remind railway servants, in a perfectly civil way, of the basic conditions of their employment. It applied, of course, only to the staff of the Great Western Railway.

Many years before railway nationalisation, however, and the ending of the individual companies, the Railway Staff Conference, which represented Britain's railwaymen as a whole, prepared and issued a small booklet called *Safety Precautions for Railway Shopmen*. It was published in 1941, with a limp red cardboard cover, and measured only 3 inches by 4 inches, so that slipping it into one's pocket presented no problem.

It can hardly have had any legal force behind it, yet the title and instructions on the front cover read:

Safety Precautions
for
Railway Shopmen
1941

The employee to whom this booklet
is supplied must retain it in his possession
and produce it when required

This must surely have been well-intentioned bluff. A workman cannot be obliged to keep a purely advisory document in his possession, nor to produce it when required. The title page is more honest. It says:

The Object
of this book is the
welfare of the
employees

it is hoped that they will
STUDY IT CAREFULLY
and act on the
recommendations
it contains

The advice given in the booklet is entirely sensible and clearly set out. It could refer to any factory and to any body of industrial workmen. It is worth quoting in its entirety, partly because it illustrates the new kind of industrial discipline which was largely brought about by the war, and partly because it is the earliest example of a manual written for the employees of every railway workshop. The workers' representatives wrote a booklet which the employers, divided as they were into separate companies, were in no position to write.

There are no fewer than 53 sections

1. First Aid

Injuries which seem trivial when they are received sometimes develop into permanent disability through septic poisoning.

On meeting with an injury, however small, go at once to an Ambulance Man or Ambulance room for treatment, even if you do not think it really necessary.

2. Accident Reports

To be paid compensation, a man must be able to prove that his injury was sustained while following his employment and arose out of his employment.

On meeting with an accident, therefore, you should at once report it to the Foreman.

3. Conduct

Many accidents occur through thoughtlessness. It is in your own interests for you always to keep your eyes open, and not to act in such a manner as is likely to cause injury to yourself or others.

4. Quarrelling, Idling, etc.

In your own interests, you should avoid idling, playing or quarrelling, as such practices frequently lead to accidents.

If an accident should result from such practices the management would take a serious view of the matter.

5. Throwing Missiles

Serious injuries may result from the throwing of missiles (coal, bread, waste, etc.), and you are warned against such a practice.

6. Leaving Work

When time for leaving work arrives you are advised to walk to the exits. If you run you may get out a second or two earlier, but you run the risk of falling over objects that may be in your path, falling owing to greasy or slippery surfaces, or colliding with other men.

7. Permitted Routes

On all occasions, use the permitted routes for getting to and from your place of work.

8. Pits

A sprained ankle or wrist or a broken rib may easily result from jumping over pits. Don't do it —walk around, or use a pit plank.

9. Lights and Lamps

Where men are not specially appointed for the duty, put out all lights before going to meals, or leaving off work.

10. Dirty Waste

Do not leave dirty or greasy waste lying around, but place it in the receptacle for such material.

11. Obstructions

Do not leave obstructions foul of the lines or on footways in shops or yards.

12. Smoking

Dropping a lighted match after lighting a pipe or cigarette may cause a fire. Lighted matches should be put out when done with. In no circumstances should smoking be indulged in in any of the woodworking shops where it is prohibited. The reason for the prohibition is the special risk of fire by reason of the inflammable nature of the materials used.

13. Inflammable Stores

To smoke, strike matches, or use naked lights in or near naphtha, petroleum or other inflammable stores, or near empty vessels which have contained inflammable liquids, is to run the risk of serious injury as well as the risk of destruction to property or material, and is therefore absolutely forbidden.

14. Fire Appliances

Special care must be taken to see that fire appliances are kept clear of all obstructions.

15. Use of Unfit Material

Do not use material that is cracked or otherwise unfit for the purpose for which it is intended as it may be a source of danger.

16. Tools

Make sure that the tools you use are in good condition and suitable for the work to be done. Defective tools, which have been supplied by the Company, can be changed at the Shop Stores.

17. Striking a File with a Hammer

Using a broken file in place of a punch is dangerous as pieces of the file sometimes fly and an eye may be lost.

18. Striking Hardened Steel

A soft hammer should be used as otherwise chips may fly off and an eye be lost.

19. Chipping

When chipping any kind of material, care should be taken to prevent the chippings from flying in the direction of other persons.

20. Guiding Saws

In starting a two-handed cross-cut saw, a block of wood is better than a hand for guiding it.

21. Ascertaining if Holes in Two Pieces of Work are Flush

Workmen sometimes use a finger to feel if holes in two pieces of work register before inserting a pin. Use a scriber or piece of wood. If you do not and the pieces of work slip you may lose your finger.

22. Use Machinery, Etc., Properly

Machinery gives best results when treated properly. In your own interests you are recommended to follow this course and to apply the same rule to all other articles you have to use.

23. Interference with Machinery

Unless an emergency or accident warrants it, no one other than the person whose ordinary employment it is may interfere with any tools or machinery, or start or stop any machine, unless specially authorised by the Foreman to do so.

24. Defects in Machinery or Workshops

A workman should call the immediate attention of a Foreman to any defect in machinery or workshops.

25. Guards on Machinery

Guards and other appliances are provided for the specific purpose of avoiding accidents. It is plain common sense to use them. Fencing guards should not be removed or kept off while the machinery is in motion. Fencing that may have been removed whilst a machine is stationary should be replaced before it is set in motion.

26. Cleaning Machinery, Etc.

If you have any regard for your own safety, you will not attempt to oil or clean moving parts of any engine, crane, or other machine, while in motion.

27. Guards of Saws

Guards are provided for the protection of the hands of the sawyer. Use them and see that they are properly adjusted to the work to be done. In the case of circular saws, see that the riving knife is also in proper position.

28. Push Sticks

Use a push stick for guiding wood being cut past the saw.

29. Moving Belts from One Pulley to Another

Do not use your hand to move belts from one pulley to another. Use a pole or stick.

30. Removing Borings, Etc.

Never try to remove borings, drillings, turnings, etc. by hand, or the hand may be cut or trapped. Always use a brush or stick. Remember also that borings, drillings, turnings, etc., are apt to stick in, or cut the fingers. Use of a brush or stick avoids this.

31. Grinding Small Articles

Keep your hands off the grindstone, or wheel, and do not attempt to grind small articles that cannot be firmly held.

32. Steam, Power and Drop Hammers

If you work in connection with steam, power, or drop hammers, do not put your hands between the hammer heads and blocks; use tongs, or else satisfy yourself that the hammer heads are properly secured or lowered on to the stop blocks provided.

Steam Hammer Drivers must not lower the hammers before getting the signal from the forgemen, and they must then satisfy themselves that everything is clear.

33. Clothing

Many a serious accident has resulted from unsuitable clothing worn by men operating lathes and other machines.

Jackets should be made to button tightly, cuffs should be provided with buttons or other means of fastening tightly round the wrist, and jackets and cuffs should be kept buttoned.

34. Eye Protectors

Eyesight is precious. Do all that you can to retain it. Use goggles on all occasions where there is the slightest risk of injury to the eye. Even if a little inconvenient, it is worth it.

If the glasses fog, this can be remedied by slightly moistening the finger and applying a film of soap to the glass, wiping off with a clean dry cloth.

35. Respirators

It is better to keep out of your system the dust that arises when grinding, buffing, and scruffing old metal work, or other dusty jobs. Use respirators; keep them clean; change the wool pads at least every day.

36. Grinding Wheels

When grinding wheels are chipped, damaged or untrue, advise the Foreman and have the wheel turned up. Rests in front of wheels should always be kept close up.

37. Hot Metal or Slag

It is dangerous to run hot metal or slag into a wet mould or ladle. See that metals are dry before being placed into a hot melting pot.

38. Standing or Crossing in front of or between Vehicles

Do not stand or pass between the buffers of vehicles standing only a short distance apart without first satisfying yourself that none of the vehicles is about to be moved by an engine, capstan, horse or other power, and that no shunting is going on upon the lines you are about to cross.

39. Work carried out on Vehicles on Lines outside Shops

It is very dangerous for men working on vehicles on running lines outside the shops to go under such vehicles without taking precautions by fixing targets or other danger signals which may be provided.

40. Moving a Vehicle (in repair shops, roads, yards, etc.)

Do not move a vehicle without first satisfying yourself that no one is engaged in any work about the vehicle or upon any other vehicle which may be affected by the moving vehicle.

41. Before crossing any line look in each direction

42. Riding on Footplates, Etc.

Unless it is absolutely necessary, do not ride on the footstep, or side footplating of an engine, whether in steam or not, or on the outside of a carriage or wagon.

43. Electrical Switchgear

Electrical Gear should be treated with great respect. Unless you are authorised to do so, do not interfere with any electrical apparatus.

No person whatsoever should operate any switch to which is attached a red 'DANGER' board.

Operators of electrically driven machines before handling the switch should see that their hands are perfectly dry.

When any work has to be done on or in such proximity to the cables or switchgear or electrical machinery that there is danger of accidental contact being made, the permission of the Shop Foreman should be obtained to have the current cut off in the section, and a 'DANGER' board should be fixed on the switch before such work is commenced.

44. Metal Rules

Metal rules should on no account be used on or near electrical switchgear that may be alive.

45. Fires on Electrical Switchboards

Do not attempt to put out a fire on an electric switchboard with a hose.

46. Putting in Electric Globes

Never put electric globes in the holder with the switch on. Lamps sometimes burst and damaged hands result.

47. Lifting Articles, Etc.
Many ruptures are caused through the legs being wide apart while lifting.
When lifting heavy articles or material, especially from the ground, keep the feet close together, slightly bend the knees, and assist in the lifting by straightening the legs.
48. Handling Panes of Glass
Panes of glass often have a razor edge, and should be held with a rag to prevent cutting the hand.
49. Dropping or Lowering Articles, Etc.
Care should be taken when dropping heavy articles from the shoulder that they do not fall where they are likely to rebound on the legs or cause other pieces of material to fly. Do not throw articles from the outside of wagons to the danger of other workmen.
50. Wagon Side Doors
Do not drop or swing open wagon side doors without ascertaining first that all is clear.
51. Oxygen and Acetylene Cylinders
The greatest care must be exercised in handling all cylinders containing gas under pressure.
52. Ladders
Make sure that the ladder you are going to use is suitable. As to whether or not a spiked ladder should be used must be determined by the nature of the surface on which the ladder is required to stand. Whenever practicable and particularly in cases of going up any considerable height, the ladder should be held at the foot and if possible secured at the top.
53. Cranes, Capstans, Lifts, Etc.
When operating a crane or capstan, or using a lift, see that you do not endanger yourself or persons nearby.

These instructions were drawn up in war-time, when both working conditions and the supply of labour were abnormal. Many workers were inexperienced, women were doing men's jobs, working hours were long and the resulting weariness caused people to make mistakes which would probably not have occurred if they had been fresh and fully awake. It was a very natural time at which to attempt to give clear, sensible advice in a form which would be readily acceptable.

We may usefully ask, however, if the management had any exact idea of how they expected this little book to be used. What kind of people, we might reasonably ask, are not aware that panes of glass have sharp edges or that it is a bad thing to drop lighted matches on the floor? Is it likely that workers who are in the habit of throwing lumps of coal at one another will be deterred by a couple of sentences in a be-sensible manual? In 1941 the railway workshops, like other factories, had to put up with employees whom they would have been unwilling to have on the premises before the war—men, women and boys whom they had not trained, and who were not used to an industrial atmosphere. Accidents were frequent, the quality of work was often indifferent and some workers would have preferred not to be there at all.

It was in this situation that a new kind of industrial relations became more or less inevitable. Much more attention had to be given to training new recruits methodically, instead of leaving them to their own devices to pick up the necessary techniques. Old practices had to be questioned, and abandoned if they appeared to be getting in the way of efficiency. Persuasion and explanation often had to take the place of orders, and in the process of getting accustomed to this a number of foremen and charge-hands discovered they had talents they would not have previously suspected. The war-years produced many welcome improvements in management-worker relationships.

They also produced a fair amount of silliness which is unfortunately still in use, and a new race of industrial-relations specialists who created a style and a jargon of their own. The fundamental difference between labour relations now and before 1939 is that today's managers are afraid of the people they control, or are trying to control, whereas yesterday's managers were firmly on top and relied ultimately on orders, not persuasion. The pendulum may possibly be swinging back again. There is something reassuring about firm orders—they provide bearings for the working day. Take it or leave it advice can be rather unsettling. One might well suppose that a worker who throws coal or lighted matches is a candidate for disciplinary action. How much damage has to be caused or how many people hurt before one decides that the offender is incapable of profiting by advice and that a firm rule would have been in everyone's best interests ?

However, for the past thirty years the climate of prejudice and opinion in industry has been increasingly permissive. The 1941 booklet quoted above is a significant fore-runner of the new age. It assumes that all workers are basically sensible and anxious to be helpful. The old rule books made no such assumption.

SINCE nationalisation, the railway works have, of course, ceased to belong to individual companies and their existing contracts of service and rules and regulations have been absorbed into the organisation and administration of British Railways, which functions as a single national unit. Within this unit, the men employed in the workshops, on construction or maintenance, have two roles. They are employees of the Railway Executive, and, as such, no different from people on the operating side, and they are industrial workers, protected by the normal factory regulations.

At a meeting of the Railway Executive held on 13 June 1949, the following resolution was passed:

That the Rules now submitted be and are hereby approved and adopted for observance by the employees of The Railway Executive from 1st January 1950, and that all former Rules which are inconsistent therewith or are made obsolete thereby shall be cancelled as from that date.

The Railway Executive subsequently became known as the British Transport Commission and the Rules, amended in various minor ways, were several times reprinted up to 1961.

They fall into two parts, the general conditions of service for all employees, no matter what their job, and the detailed rules to be observed by men actually engaged in running trains. The first part, described as *Extracts from Rule Book, 1950*, is issued as a separate little booklet to all new recruits, with this note: 'Each employee supplied with this book must make himself acquainted with, and will be held responsible for the observance of, the following rules.'

'All employees', says Rule 1(a),

must reside at whatever place may be appointed, attend at such hours as may be required, promptly obey persons placed in authority over them, and conform to all the Rules and Regulations of the Railway Executive.

They may be required to 'join any Fund or Society established by the Railway Executive for the benefit of its staff as may be appropriate', undergo medical examinations and, if they hold positions of trust, 'find security for their faithful services'. An exact repeat of a Great Western Rule of 1933. Under Rule 1(h),

When an employee leaves the service he must immediately deliver up his uniform and all other articles belonging to the Railway Executive. Any pay due to the employee leaving the service will not be paid until the uniform and all other articles the property of the Railway Executive, supplied to him, shall have been delivered up or satisfactorily accounted for. If any article be not delivered up, be missing, or be damaged by improper use, the value of such article, or the cost of the repair of such damage, shall be a debt due from the employee to the Railway Executive, and may (subject to the provisions of the Truck Acts) be deducted from any pay then due, or, if such pay be found insufficient to meet the claim, will become a debt re-coverable at law.

Their working brains belong to their employer, as Rule 1(i) makes clear:

Employees must comply with the Regulations of the British Transport Commission with regard to the patenting of inventions and registration of designs made or discovered in the course of their employment or by means of facilities enjoyed by means of their employment.

The employer's right to discipline is spelt out in Rule 4:

The Railway Executive may at any time:—
(i) dismiss without notice, or
(ii) suspend from duty and, after enquiry, dismiss without notice, or
(iii) suspend from duty, as a disciplinary measure
an employee of the Railway Executive for any one or more of the following offences:—
(a) drunkenness,
(b) disobedience of orders,
(c) misconduct or negligence,
(b) absence from duty without leave.
An employee so dismissed forfeits any rights to notice and also any right to wages for any period subsequent to his dismissal or his suspension from duty prior to dismissal as the case may be.
An employee suspended from duty pending enquiry and not exonerated, if not dismissed, may as part of his punishment awarded be deprived of any or all of the wages accruing to him in respect of the period of his suspension as to the Railway Executive may seem just and reasonable.
An employee suspended from duty as a disciplinary measure forfeits any right to wages for the period of his suspension.

When travelling by train, staff must keep themselves to themselves:

Workmen of the Railway, holding passes or free tickets, when going to or from their work, must travel together, and, as far as possible, apart from other passengers. When compartments are reserved for their use, they must ride in these compartments only.

Apart from enforcing these general regulations, the main post-war concern of British Railways, in running the workshops, has been with safety. To drive home the safety message the usual 'watch it' type of industrial safety posters have been used, but in addition the Commission has gone to a good deal of trouble to produce special booklets. These are written in the chatty 'let's face it' style nowadays considered appropriate for talking to the people for whom one is responsible and who are likely to leave at the end of the week or go on strike if they feel they are being patronised, bullied or insulted in any way. The difference in approach between these booklets and the pre-war Rules and Regulations marks a revolution in industrial relations.

In 1961 British Railways issued a pamphlet called *Your Personal Safety—Workshop Staff*. It had a green cover, with a symbolic man holding a symbolic triangle, and it was generously illustrated with coloured drawings.

Inside the front cover is printed:

NAME
CHECK OR CLOCK NUMBER
This booklet is issued to help you protect yourself and your mates from injury. Take good care of it and make yourself familiar with the advice it gives. You will be asked to produce it for inspection from time to time.
When you receive it, fill in your name and clock or check number in the space provided on the inside front cover. You should also fill in the separate acknowledgment form and hand it in. It will be attached to your employment papers.
If you should lose the booklet, tell your Supervisor immediately.

The message is simple and personal:

Let's face it, a busy railway workshop can be a dangerous place. When you've been round a bit, you begin to learn by personal experience. But it could be too late. How much better to gain by the experience of others!

Records over many years show that time and time again the same kinds of accidents happen in the workshops; they reveal, too, that most of them are caused by carelessness.

Carelessness often means the loss of a limb or an eye; and sometimes a life. You have to be careful all the time about everything you do and in everything you do and in every move you make. Another thing—the more safety-conscious everybody is, the less likely are you to suffer by your mates' carelessness, and they by yours. Safety is a team job.

Now is the time for you to say, "I'll make sure it doesn't happen to *me* !"

The purpose of this booklet is to pass on to you for your personal safety the accumulated experience gained by countless railway shopmen in over a century of railway working. It cannot possibly cover every source of danger or accident. But those who have compiled it sincerely hope that a study of it will make you more 'safety conscious' and so save you, your mates, and those near and dear to you much pain and suffering.

'Safety regulations,' it goes on, 'are there to help in protecting you from injury. Certain of them, required by the Factories Acts, are made for the protection of you and your mates against accident or ill-health, and you will find a summary of them posted on the notice-boards; read it carefully. Read particularly the regulations which apply to your own job, and, what is more important, keep to them.'

The warnings cover much the same range of foolish behaviour as the 1941 booklet, *Safety Precautions for Railway Shopmen*, which has already been quoted, but a comparison between the two shows an increase in the conversational flavour. There are messages which must somehow get across for both legal and humanitarian reasons:

Fooling About—cut out the fooling. Every day, people get injured through playing around, quarrelling or throwing things about.

Knocking-off Time—when it is time to leave your work, walk to the exit. If you run you may get out a little earlier, but you take the risk of tripping over things in your way, slipping on a greasy patch, or colliding with other men.

Power and Drop Hammers—If you work with power or drop hammers, do not put your hands or any part of your body between the hammer-head and the block. Use tongs or else make quite sure that the hammer-head is properly secured or lowered on to the stop-block or prop. Hammer-drivers must not lower the hammers before getting the signal from the responsible operator, and they must satisfy themselves that everything is clear.

Interference with Machinery—Do not use machinery, plant or tools which you are not authorised and competent to operate. If you interfere with machinery you are unfamiliar with, you may hurt yourself or cause one of your mates to be injured. Report defects to your supervisor.

Cold Chisels and Sets—Do not use chisels or cold sets with burred-over or mushroomed heads. Far too many accidents, particularly to eyes, are caused by this. Hardening of these tools can be done only by qualified staff with special apparatus.

We are in the modern world, in which factory workers have to be specifically told that grease is slippery and that power-hammers are not good for any hands that get in the way and in which motorists are not aware of fog or ice unless there is an illuminated sign to tell them it is officially foggy or icy.

By 1968 the ad-men are firmly in control. The current booklet,[1] *Sense and Safety in the Workshop*, produced for the Board's Accident Prevention Service, is a delightful piece of work, full of witty cartoons of railwaymen in hospital, railwaymen throwing lighted matches in the direction of gas cylinders, railwaymen busy giving one another electric

F

shocks, falling down holes and rupturing themselves by lifting heavy weights in the wrong way. The modern theory appears to be that, in our advertisement-soaked world, nobody pays attention to anybody unless they are amused at the same time, an idea which would have seemed absurd to the autocrats who drew up the nineteenth-century rule books. 'The moving parts of any Engine, Crane, Lathe or other machine, must not be oiled or cleaned whilst in motion' emphasised the 1904 Swindon Rules. 'A workman who violates any provision of this will be considered guilty of serious and wilful misconduct, and to have rendered himself liable to instant dismissal.'

'Wouldn't life be a lot nicer if there were no accidents ?', begins *Sense and Safety in the Workshop* in 1968. 'We'd do away with lots of pain; lots of shock and grief; lots of tears; lots of sheer downright inconvenience and nuisance—and lots of hardship.' Fifty or a hundred years earlier this would have been regarded as sentimental rubbish, which indeed it is. The old-style factory-worker was told what to do and what not to do. If he chopped his hands off by being clumsy or by ignoring safety precautions, that was his fault. The man in industry today has to be wheedled and persuaded to behave sensibly, or so it seems to be believed, and so we have the matey presentation of *Sense and Safety in the Workshop, 1968*. It advises and reasons. Orders are undemocratic and out of date. We quote it in full to complete the story.

Wouldn't life be a lot nicer if there were no accidents?

We'd do away with lots of pain; lots of shock and grief; lots of tears; lots of sheer downright inconvenience and nuisance—and lots of hardship.

The dictionary calls an accident 'an event without apparent cause.' Well, of course, there's always a cause—sometimes obvious and sometimes not so obvious.

We're all only human and we can't see round corners. What we can do is to try really hard not to help accidents happen through thoughtlessness and carelessness.

A lot of people have worked hard to devise safety rules for your job. Please give them a 'thank you' by taking their very good advice.

Don't be a Charlie!

OK, OK, so you know how to look after yourself. You're not such a Charlie as to chop your thumb off or something.

But just a minute. Haven't you ever taken a bit of a chance now and then and thought afterwards that it was a dicey thing to do?

Haven't you sometimes had your mind on something else when your own experience tells you that you need all your concentration on a tricky job?

Think, now. You're not all that lucky on the Pools, or picking a 'cert' for the 3.30. So don't tempt Lady Luck at work; that's for Charlies who don't know when they're on a loser.

If you don't think this booklet is full of sound common sense—we'll, see you (and Charlie) on visiting day!

Safe ways

Don't kid yourself that there's no danger at all in your job. Even station announcers get laryngitis! The great thing is not to get cocksure and careless. You know the safe way—be sensible and stick to it.

The track

Ever seen the silent films? Heroine tied to the rails; the 6.15 approaching fast and honest Tom setting her free at the last second? Strictly for the trick cameramen this one. You can't judge the speed of an approaching train—so keep off the track unless you must be there. Even at ¼-mile distance you've got to step really lively to get clear. Electrified lines don't even need trains to kill you. Keep well away.

Equipment

You wouldn't wander into the pilot's cabin of a Jumbo Jet and decide to test your theories on quick take-offs. So don't push your luck with equipment, machinery or vehicles you're not supposed to handle.

Faulty equipment or anything you think might cause an accident is your business—but definitely.

Report it. Get it put right.

Conduct

So Charlie clowns around and everyone thinks he's a right laugh. Ever noticed how often skylarking gets out of hand until some poor innocent mutt gets hurt? When you're at work, use your head and keep a sense of proportion.

Fire

Please, be serious about fire risks. So you're dying for a quick drag and there's a dirty great NO SMOKING sign on the wall. Do yourself a good turn and keep it for later. It'll save you money, cure your cough and maybe avoid a really nasty flare-up with a lot of people getting hurt.

In particular, be specially careful in warehouses, storerooms, near gas cylinders or inflammable liquids. Never leave clothing, sacking, waste, wood shavings or anything burnable near fires, stoves or stovepipes.

If, in spite of everything, Charlie insists on sitting in the fuel store and rubbing two sticks together in his best Boy Scout manner—

know your fire instructions

know where fire-fighting equipment is kept;

know how to use it.

Slips and falls

Ever noticed how your first impulse is to laugh when someone trips or falls off a chair or something?

Well, it's not so funny if you're the unlucky one—especially if you twist awkwardly and find yourself in the 'slipped disc' brigade. That can be a long, painful job, as we all know.

F*

So, look where you're going. Don't go mountaineering over obstacles or pot-holing down pits and excavations, and watch out for

slippery patches—grit or sand them;

litter or debris—remove it;

rough or uneven surfaces—tread warily.

Remedy these hazards if you can, otherwise report them.

Take extra care when getting on or off vehicles. And if it's dark, leave the night-vision demonstrations to the cat. You take a handlamp.

Manhandling

There's plenty of scope for doing yourself a mischief. So you're a big, strong, man-mountain. You'll still wind up in Ward 10 having a funny operation if you try to pick up a heavy, awkward crate in a careless way. Now here are some really good hints which will even keep the show-offs out of trouble.

Do yourself a real favour and read them.

Lifting and carrying

1. Size up the job.
   Obstructions, greasy floors?
   Sharp edges, nails?
   If too heavy, get help.
2. Stand firmly.
   Close to load, feet about 12 inches apart. One foot ahead of the other in direction of move.
3. Bend the knees.
   Keep your back straight.
   Chin well in.
4. Get a firm grip.
   Use whole of fingers, not just the tips. Keep load close to body.
   Grip diagonally.
5. Lift with your legs.
   Lift by straightening legs. Use impetus of lift to move off in direction required.
6. Putting things down.
   Back straight. Legs bend. Avoid trapped fingers—put load down askew, slide into position.

Heaving

1. Tuck chin in.
2. Keep back and arms straight.
3. Bend front knee to allow body to move back.
4. Thrust with front leg.
5. Back foot maintains balance.

Pushing

1. Tuck chin in.
2. Keep back and arms straight.
3. Thrust with rear foot, pointing forwards.
4. Front foot forwards to maintain balance.

Accidents must be reported

No matter how trivial, tell your supervisor. Otherwise you may have difficulty in proving any claim for personal injury benefit.

Tidiness

If you've ever trodden on the upturned teeth of a rake and been whacked on the nose as the handle leaps upwards, you'll agree that it's no better than walking into a ladder in a dark passage or having your toes mangled by a runaway roller. Make it easy for yourself and your mates by putting tools and equipment where they belong. Keep footpaths, walking routes and working places clear of spoil and spillage, materials and freight.

Authorised routes

There are authorised walking routes which have been agreed with your local representatives as the safest way to go. We all know about the clever types who think it's smart to take short cuts across the tracks and so on. But what's so smart about it? A better word is lazy, or stupid; but clever, never!

Electricity is a killer

The trouble with electrical equipment is that it looks so innocent and harmless. But beware, you amateur electricians. It packs a punch that'll do more than just burn your fingers. So leave the handling of electrical apparatus to those qualified to do the job. Even they are reminded of these obvious and simple rules:

Never adjust or repair electrical apparatus unless you have isolated it from the main supply.

Never plug or unplug equipment without first switching off at the appliance and at the socket.

Make sure that your hands are dry.

Loose connections and worn or frayed cables are dangerous. Report them.

Clothing

"Pop star mauled by screaming fans" might make a good newspaper story. But long hair, torn clothing and untied shoelaces can really be a danger if you're working near machinery. Anyway, who wants to look like a scarecrow, when you can get such a lift out of being clean and tidy as well as being dressed suitably for the job?

If you are issued with High Visibility clothing, always wear it when at work, and keep it clean so that it can do its job.

Protective gear

Footwear, gloves, goggles, bump cap —if any of these are provided because of some particular health or injury hazard in your job—*use them.*

First Aid

If you suffer an injury, however slight, don't just laugh it off, seek treatment from a trained First Aider.

First Aid saves lives

More trained First Aiders are needed. If you've ever fancied yourself as a budding Dr. Kildare—act now! Ask your supervisor for details.

THE TOOLS OF YOUR TRADE

If you've had a bit of a giggle reading this booklet so far, well, that's fine. When all's said and done a little bit of sugar helps the medicine go down! As long as you've got the message, that's the thing.

From here on, though, we're switching off the jolly stuff. So the notes that follow are straight from the lecture-room. But no matter how long you've been at the job you'll find it well worth your while to read on to the end. Bet you'll finish up just a bit more safety-conscious — and that's to everybody's benefit . . . except Charlie's!

The right tool for the job. The right use for every tool.

Only tools in good condition are safe and only the right tool properly used gets the job done safely.

Be tidy in the use of tools and when the job is finished stow them away safely. That's craftsmanship — and it's safe.

Hand tools

Examine regularly; if defective send them in for repair or replacement.

Point the cutting face of edged tools away from your hands or body.

Never attempt heat treatment of tools unless you are authorised.

Repairs must be carried out only by an authorised person.

Chipping

When chipping any metal, prevent flying chippings from injuring others, if necessary use screens.

Hammers

Hammers should not be used if:

the head is worn or chipped;

the head is loose on the shaft;

the shaft is split or broken.

If your hammer is oily or greasy wipe it before use. Don't strike a steel hammer against another or on any other hardened metal. Flying metal fragments can blind people.

Cold chisels or sets

Do not use cold chisels or sets if heads are split or mushroomed or the cutting edges are defective. Keep heads free of oil, grease and dirt.

Files

Never use a file without a handle; the smallest of slips may drive the tang into your hand.

Your file is not a punch or a lever. The hardened steel of which it is made is very brittle and snaps easily.

Spanners

Use the correct spanner for the job.

Do not use open-end spanners which are splayed or ring spanners which are deformed.

Check adjustable spanners or monkey-wrenches for excessive play.

Never use improvised extension handles for extra leverage.

Nuts may 'give' suddenly, so be careful when undoing them. Pull rather than push.

Your spanner is not a hammer; don't use it as one.

Screwdrivers

Use the correct size for the job.

Never use a screwdriver if the handle is split or the working end damaged.

A screwdriver is not a chisel or lever so don't use a hammer on it. Mind your other hand—the screwdriver might slip.

Saws

Wood Saws

Carry saws with the teeth covered.

Use a block of wood and not your hand when starting the cut.

Hacksaws

Use the correct type of blade, stretched tightly in the frame. Use the saw in a straight line with light strokes to avoid breaking the blade.

Rods or drifts

Use a metal rod, drift, bar or pin to check the alignment of holes— not your finger.

MACHINERY

Moving machinery

Never clean, oil or adjust until all parts are stationary, and then only if you are authorised.

To move a belt from one pulley to another use a pole stick—not your hand.

Take care never to distract anyone who is operating a machine.

Fencing and guards

Fencing and guards prevent accidents. Never remove them when the machine is working.

Before operating the machine see that all guards are in position and if one is missing or you think that it is not correctly adjusted or is defective tell your supervisor.

Grindstones and abrasive wheels

Keep hands clear of abrasive surfaces.

Don't try to grind articles that are too small to hold firmly. File them instead.

Keep work rests close up in front of grinding wheels. Report excessive clearance.

Report wheels that are chipped or out of true. Don't try to remedy them unless you are authorised.

Protect your eyes with goggles.

Power saws

Ensure all guards are in position and correctly adjusted to the thickness of the wood being sawn before operating.

Use a push-stick to feed the material past the saw blade.

Never try to remove an obstruction unless the blade is stationary.

Power hammers and drop-forging machines

Don't get any part of your body between the hammerhead and the block. Hold the job with tongs.

If the blocks have to be adjusted, either secure the hammerhead ¦or lower it on to stop brackets or a prop.

Operators—ensure others are not in a position of possible danger.

Power presses

All guards must be in position and functioning correctly.

Setting and adjusting of tools must only be undertaken by someone who is authorised.

Cranes

Cranes must only be operated by those authorised. The signals must be given by one recognised person.

Always operate a crane within its capacity and use the lifting tackle of correct type and capacity.

Clothing and tidiness

Moving machinery can catch hold of anything loose, torn or untidy, so tuck everything in and button everything up.

As for your hair, keep it short or keep it under your hat.

General

Use a brush, or stick to clear away borings, drillings or turnings.

Any machinery you are not authorised or competent to use—leave alone.

ELECTRICAL APPARATUS

Treat all apparatus with respect and don't interfere with it.

If you see defects such as damaged switch covers, frayed or defective cable insulation—report them but don't try to repair unless you are qualified.

If you get a shock, however slight, report it. The apparatus is faulty.

Before oiling or adjusting a power-driven appliance—switch off.

Never touch a switch with a DANGER board or CAUTION notice on it.

Before working on or near electrical equipment, if there is danger of accidental contact, get a 'Permit to work'.

Never use improvised plugs.

Never handle electrical equipment with wet hands.

Portable tools

Don't leave them running unnecessarily. Avoid running the cable where it may be damaged, and when the job is finished or interrupted for a period, switch off at the supply point and recoil the cable.

Electric lamps

Switch off before removing or inserting a lamp or tube in its holder.

Substations and testing areas

If you are not authorised to enter a substation or test area when the barriers are in position or testing is in progress—keep out.

Radiography

Keep away from areas where x-rays or sealed radiation sources are used.

Fire

If there is a fire in or near electrical equipment get the current switched off.

Extinguishers for electrical fires are marked with a two-inch yellow band.

Do not use water, water 'gas pressure' foam or soda-acid types of extinguishers until the current has been switched off.

Electric shock

Never touch the victim with bare hands if he is still in contact with the live supply. If you can, switch off at once; if not, move the victim clear, using a piece of wood or dry cloth, or pull him clear with a length of dry rope.

Give First Aid immediately.

HIGH-PRESSURE GASES AND LIQUIDS

You can be seriously injured or die if compressed gas gets into your body or bloodstream. Cover any open wound. Never direct a pressure jet at anyone. This includes high-pressure liquid, i.e. paint (spraying) and diesel oil fuel (injectors).

Cylinders must not be dropped or allowed to knock together or hit other objects.

Tell the supervisor immediately you find that a cylinder is overheated.

Do not change cylinders of 'snift' valves near naked lights.

Never mix gases in a cylinder or transfer gas from one cylinder to another.

Never test for leaks with a flame.

Don't let any oil, grease or combustible material come into contact with cylinders, valves, regulators or fittings.

Keep cylinders away from any source of heat.

Protect the valves against damage and open and close them slowly.

Do not use leaking or bad connections.

Make sure you know the instructions.

Oxy-gas cutting and welding

Read the instructions and obey them.

Make sure the equipment is in good order.

Use any protective equipment provided (i.e. apron, goggles or eye-shield); remember that welding flash ('arc-eye') can damage your sight. Use screens if necessary to protect others from 'flash' or flying sparks.

Make sure no inflammable material is lying near enough to be ignited by sparks.

Make sure no sparks or hot particles are left smouldering after the work is finished.

Blowlamps

Don't use the wrong fuel.

Don't place a blowlamp on or near a stove.

Don't use one blowlamp to heat up another.

Don't interfere with the safety valve or other working parts. If the lamp is faulty, send it for repairs.

LADDERS, WALKWAYS, SCAFFOLDING & ROOF SURFACES

Ladders

1. Use the right ladder for the job.
2. Place securely on even ground, pitching four up—one out.
3. Lash it or foot it.
4. Watch out for live overhead cables.
5. Grip it with both hands.
6. Don't over-reach; move the ladder.
7. Carry with the front end raised.

Never use step-ladders as supports for planking.

Handrails

Handrails should be held—not leant on! They must not be used to support loads.

Roofs

Always use permanent walkways.

Never cross a roof without using a portable roof ladder or crawling boards which reach across the roof supports.

Mobile scaffolding units must be secured when in use and should not be moved.

Other structures, poles, posts, etc.

Before climbing, ensure they are safe, particularly if not stayed. Test for decay by striking with a hammer or inserting a knife.

When working up a telegraph pole, use a safety belt.

PROTECTING YOUR BODY

Eyes

Never do anything that will endanger your sight. Use every means to protect your eyes. Goggles will protect them from flying pieces and from fumes and splashes when you are handling acids or caustic soda. Ask your supervisor for a pair for your personal use.

To avoid 'fogging', moisten your finger, apply a film of soap to the inside of the lens and wipe off with a clean, dry cloth.

Ears

Excessive noise can damage your hearing. Protect with earplugs or muffs.

Hands

Make sure your hands are protected when you handle hot material, acids, glass or other sharp articles.

Lungs

Don't damage your health where there are dust and fumes. If you are provided with a respirator, wear it.

Feet

Don't leave nails sticking out of timbers where they can be trodden on; knock them down.

Sensible people wear the right shoe for every occasion. For doing your job—the Safety Shoe or Boot with steel toecaps and insoles to protect you against knocks and falling articles. See your local footwear agent.

GOING ABOUT ...
Inspection pits
Don't jump over a pit; you could sprain an ankle or wrist or break a rib. Use a plank or walk round.
Red flags, targets and 'Not to be moved' boards
If you have to work on vehicles outside the Shops, don't go underneath unless red flags or targets are displayed.
Working on vehicles
Always use a scotch. The slightest movement could trap you.

Keep your legs and feet clear of the wheels.

When lifting vehicles use packing and trestles.

When getting into or out of a vehicle mind you don't tread on any loose or insecure object.

When climbing into a wagon don't tread on the buffer spindle. Place your foot on the guide.
Wagon doors
When opening wagon doors, stand well clear. When closing them, fasten them securely or someone else may be injured.

Before starting work on a wagon make sure the door is securely fastened.
Capstan and traverser ropes
Stand well clear when these are in use.
Crossing lines
Look both ways before crossing any line—even a siding in the Works —just as you would when crossing a main road.

Don't forget that one train can hide another.

Never try to pass between vehicles that are being shunted.

Always use authorised crossings. Pick your feet up! Step over rails and not on them.
Heavy articles
When lowering or stacking these, put rather than throw or drop. Be careful that they do not bounce back on to you, hit your mate, or cause other articles to fly up.
Suspended loads
Never walk or stand under a load suspended from an overhead crane or magnet.
Working inside boilers, tanks or other large containers
Make sure everyone concerned knows you are there.
Excavations
Never work in deep excavations or unstable ground unless the sides are well shuttered.

Never stand material near the edges of excavations: the earth might collapse and injure men working below.

Cycling
Only ride along paths where this is permitted.
Going home
Don't rush—having kept yourself safe all day, don't get hurt on the way home.

In the early years of this century men walked two hours each way to and from their work in Crewe and Swindon. Nobody said to them, 'Don't get hurt on the way home'. It was not felt to be part of an employer's function to give this kind of advice. A man was responsible for himself.

Today's pieces of advice—they can hardly be called rules—are written in two distinct styles. Neither appears intended to be read quickly and privately. What the author has really produced is something to be read aloud to an audience, a film commentary or a television script, words to be spoken while the person being addressed is looking at the pictures.

Much of this booklet is pure commentary, composed for people who are used to taking information through their ears, rather than their eyes.

Think now. You're not all that lucky on the Pools or picking a cert for the 3.30. So don't tempt Lady Luck at work; it's all for Charlies who don't know when they're on a loser.

and

There's plenty of scope for doing yourself a mischief. So you're a big, strong, man-mountain. You'll still wind up in Ward 10 having a funny operation if you try to pick up a heavy, awkward crate in a careless way. Now here are some really good lines which will even keep the show-offs out of trouble. Do yourself a real favour and read them.

There is, however, another spoken style in this booklet, in the staccato, headlining, ultra-economic style of the Army drill-sergeant:

Use whole of fingers, not just the tip. Keep load close to body.

and

Don't get any part of your body between the hammerhead and the block.

Nowadays, British Railways have access to the accumulated wisdom of industrial psychologists and of specialists in industrial relations. They must, one assumes have taken the best advice before committing themselves to a publication of this kind. And yet one wonders if this chatty picture-filled text is really any more effective than the sharp, unfriendly, nineteenth-century rules. The only measure of effectiveness is whether people's behaviour is changed to any significant extent. Have accidents gone down ? Do people arrive more punctually ? Do they steal less ? It is no great problem to compare one year's figures with another's and to say whether the results are better or worse than they were twelve months ago. What is extremely difficult is to pin down the reasons for an improvement. Is it better supervision, better training, better plant layout and safety precautions, the welcome disappearance of a few notoriously accident-prone employees, shorter working hours, less overtime, or the weather ? Or have these booklets and posters just possibly got something to do with it ? The people responsible for them will naturally say yes, as anyone involved in the advertising or public-relations business is bound to, if he is hoping for more work in the future.

The employer can only hope for the best. He may not really believe that a booklet like this does much good, but he can't be sure, so he agrees with the communications experts. And, in any case, if an accident does occur, he can always point to the advice that the man was given in print and publicise the fact that it wasn't followed. Morally and legally he is in the clear. The nineteenth-century manager or factory owner would probably find it difficult to understand his state of mind.

APPENDICES

RULES OF THE SERVANTS' HALL AT HATCHLANDS

In the Servants' Hall at Hatchlands, in Surrey, built by Admiral Boscawen in 1759 and now the property of the National Trust, the Rules and Orders still survive on their original 4 feet by 3 feet framed board. They may quite possibly have been drawn up by the Admiral himself. It is not fanciful, perhaps, to see something of a quarter-deck manner about them.

'RULES and ORDERS, to be OBSERV'D in this HALL, without EXCEPTION

1. Whoever is left at Breakfast, to clear the Table, and put the Copper horns, Salt, Pepper, &c in their proper places.. or forfeit   3d.

2. That the Postilion & Groom shall have the Servants hall cloth laid for Dinner by one o'clock and not omit laying Salt, Pepper, spoons, &c ....   3d.

3. That the knives for Dinner, and the housekeeper's room, to be clean'd ev'ry day by the Postilion and Groom, and in case one is out the other do his business in his absence, be it which it may ....   3d.

4. That if any Person be heard to swear, or use any indecent language at any time when the Cloth is on the Table ....   3d.

5. Whoever leaves any powder or pomatum, or any thing belonging to their dress, or any wearing apparel, out of their proper places ....   3d.

6. That no one be suffer'd to play at cards in this Hall, between six in the Morning and six in the Evening ......   3d.

7. Whoever leaves any pieces of Bread at breakfast, Dinner, or Supper ....   1d.

8. That if any one should be detected cleaning liverys, Cloaths, or leather Breeches, at any time of meals, or shall leave any dirt after cleaning them, at any time ...   3d.

9. That the Postilion and Groom have the Hall decently swept, and the dirt taken away before Dinner time ...   3d.

10. That every servant shall assist to pump Water for the use of the House, every Wednesday .... 3d.

11. That no one shall put any kind of Provision in any Cupboard or Drawer in the hall after their meals, but shall return it from whence they had it .... 3d.

12. That the Table cloth shall after all meals be folded up and put in the Drawer for that purpose .... 3d.

13. That if any one be detected wipeing their knives in the Table cloth at any time .... 3d.

14. That if any stable, or other servant, take any plates to the stable, or be seen to set them for dogs to eat off ...... 6d.

15. That no wearing apparel, or hat boxes, be suffered to hang in the Hall but shall be put in the closets for that purpose .... 3d.

Whoever defaces these R U L E S, in any manner

shall forfeit 5/6d.

APPENDIX II

SAFETY RULES OF THE ROYAL GUNPOWDER FACTORY,
FAVERSHAM

The earliest known industrial safety rules were drawn up in 1785, for the benefit of workers at what must have been at that time the most dangerous factory in Britain, the Royal Gunpowder Factory at Faversham. They are clear and sensible and served as a basis for all future rules in the industry. The workers had good reason to observe them, if they had any wish to remain alive.

1. If any workman belonging to the Royal Mills wears his slippers out of those parts of the Works where they are intended to be used for safety, or wears his own shoes into any of the said works, any such workman is to be chequed a day's pay for the first offence and if they should so far forget the duty they owe their country as a second time to run the risque of blowing the works up through such negligence they are to be discharged and on no account to be entered again.

2. The respective officers will please to give the strictest orders for having the several works cleaned out whenever they require it, and the cleaning is not to be confined to the floors only but to every part of the machinery and buildings to prevent any accumulation of dust, which in a powder manufactory must be attended with the greatest danger.

3. The hinges of all doors and window shutters are to be kept well oiled, also the pulleys over which the window lines go and the grooves in which the sashes slide to be brushed and scraped as often as occasion requires to prevent any dangerous friction. The cogs, axles and other parts of the machinery to be kept well soaped and oiled as has hitherto been the custom.

4. The pulleys belonging to the valves of the power stoves must be carefully examined and if there is a possibility of the ropes rubbing against wood or if the sheaves of the pulleys are made of wood they must be altered, so that the ropes may rub against copper, and the sheaves be made of the same metal.

5. Whenever the powder tumbrils are required to come near a building in which powder is contained, brick rubbish must be laid on the ground after it has been very carefully examined that no flint or other stones remain therein.

6. Each of the corning houses are to be completed with canvas receivers in the dust troughs and a canvas curtain similar to that ordered for No. 1 corning house.

7. When barrels of gunpowder are lifted out of boats to be stored in the magazines or powder vessels, the strictest attention must be paid to have them brushed all over with a soft brush to prevent any grit hanging to them. The wheelbarrows on which they are to be carried, the hold of the vessel in which it is to be laid to be cleaned in the same manner.

8. All the wheelbarrows which are used to carry powder are to be fitted with copper hoops and gudgeons instead of iron.

9. The floors of the cooperage must be kept as clean from sand or gravel as the magazine and the coopers must work in their magazine slippers to prevent any grit adhering to the barrels or charge tubs, and before any of the articles are issued from the cooperage they must be well brushed and cleaned.

London and North Western Railway.

RULES

OF THE

Wolverton Works Fire Brigade.

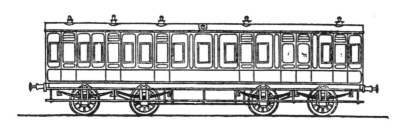

GENERAL INSTRUCTIONS

FOR THE

WOLVERTON WORKS FIRE BRIGADE.

THE following instructions are to be considered as
General Regulations, but not containing rules of conduct
applicable to every variety of circumstances that may
occur to individuals in the performance of their duty.
It will therefore be incumbent upon the men to render
prompt and cheerful obedience to the commands of their
superiors; to execute their duty as steadily and quietly
as possible; to be careful not to annoy the inhabitants
of houses they may be called upon to enter; to treat all
persons with civility; to take care to preserve presence
of mind and good temper, and not to allow themselves
to be distracted from their duty by the advice or
directions of any persons but their own officers, and
to observe the strictest sobriety and general regularity
of behaviour.

The conditions upon which each man is admitted
into the Wolverton Works Fire Brigade are stated here,

3

so that no complaint may be made hereafter upon their being enforced. The Company desire it to be understood at the same time that they reserve to themselves the power to alter or annul any of the conditions, and also to make such new Rules as may be found expedient. Each man shall devote his whole time when called upon duty, and not leave until discharged by his Superintendent or the officer in command, and shall reside in houses provided by the Company for Firemen. Each man shall receive, as occasion may require, one body coat, (marked with the No. answering to his name in the books) one pair of trousers, one hat, or other covering for the head, one belt, one screw key, one small axe, and one lamp.

Each man in the service is liable to immediate dismissal for drunkenness, unfitness, negligence, or misconduct; any man destroying his equipments, or wearing them when off duty, will be punished by fines or dismissal from the service, as the Superintendent may determine. Careless conduct, irregular attendance at exercise, or disobedience of superior officer's commands, to be punished as above.

THE SUPERINTENDENT

shall reside as near the Works as possible. The moment an alarm of fire is given he will attend with the Engine and Firemen, and have the entire direction thereof, and shall employ such additional hands as may be necessary. He will endeavour to ascertain the cause of the Fire, and report the same to the Company. He must be firm and just, but, at the same time, kind and conciliatory in his

4

behaviour on all occasions. He must give clear and precise instructions to the men under him. Every instance of neglect or disobedience must be reported to his superiors, and punished by fines, &c. At a fire he will also take command of any men and engines not belonging to the Company which may come to his assistance in case of need, and be careful to place the engines in such a position that the men working at the levers may be in no danger from falling of premises.

DUTY OF CAPTAIN.

He will reside as near the Works as possible, and obey all orders given to him by the Superintendent when any of the men are absent after an alarm of fire is given, and will be responsible for any misconduct of the men when he fails to report such misconduct to the Superintendent. He must see that the Engines are always kept in good order, and report to the Superintendent when any part of the apparatus is in need of repair, and never allow any man unaccompanied to enter a building on fire.

DUTY OF SERGEANTS:

The Sergeant will take command in the absence of the Captain. When the Captain is present the Sergeant will give him all possible assistance in conducting the Engine to the fire ; and it will be more particularly his duty to see that the Engine is supplied with water, and that every man is at his

5

station, and he must remain with his Engine while on duty whether working or not, unless he receives special orders to the contrary. Before leaving the Engine House on the return from a fire, and at the conclusion of every drill, he must see that all appliances are in good order and in their proper position ready for work. Any defect must be immediately reported to the Senior Officer present.

PIONEERS.

When the alarm of Fire is given, the two Firemen arriving first at the Engine House must act as Pioneers, and proceed at once to the place where the fire is, in order to prepare for the arrival of the Engine and make ready the most available supply of water. They must also examine the state of the premises on fire and the neighbouring ones, so as to be able to give such information to the Captain as may enable him to apply his force to the best advantage. When the Engines arrive, the Pioneers will fall in with the Brigade, and take their further instructions from the Captain.

FIREMEN.

On the alarm of Fire being given, the whole Brigade, Pioneers excepted, must assemble as speedily as possible at the Engine House, properly equipped in the established uniform, and act with spirit under the orders of their Officers in getting everything ready for service. As nothing is so hurtful to the efficiency of an establishment for the extinguishing of fires as unnecessary

6

noise, irregularity or insubordination, it is enjoined on all to observe quietness and regularity, to execute readily whatever orders they may receive from their Officers, and do nothing without orders. All the Firemen must be particularly careful to let the Policemen on their respective beats know where they reside, and take notice when the Policeman is changed, that they may give the new one the requisite information. The men are particularly cautioned not to take spirituous liquors from any individual without the special permission of the Captain, who will see that every proper and necessary refreshment be afforded to them, as intoxication on such alarming occasions is not only disreputable to the Brigade, but in the highest degree dangerous, by rendering the men unfit for their duty. Every appearance of it will be most rigidly marked, and any member who may be discovered in that state shall not only forfeit his whole allowance for the turn out and duty performed, but will be forthwith dismissed from the Brigade.

The Captain, whose duty it is to see that the Engines are ready for action, should be near the Branchmen to direct them, receiving his instructions from his Superintendent.

The man who holds the Branch-pipes gives orders for such a number of lengths of Hose as may be required.

The Sub-branchman's duties are similar to the Branchman's, taking his position in his absence or relieving

7

him at the Branch, or when two deliveries are playing he should take the second.

The Firemen should be numbered from 1 upwards.

When the line of operation is decided upon, and water obtained, No. 6 is to mount the Engine and give out the hose, the Branchman taking out the Branch-pipe; No. 3 takes the first length of hose which he screws to the delivery of the engine and uncoils it in the direction of the fire where the Branchman takes his attacking position; No. 4 receives another length of hose, screws it on to No. 3; Nos. 5, 6, and 7 act the same way until a sufficient length of hose has been obtained; Nos. 8, 9, and 10 screw the suction pipes with rose on the Engine. One man should look to the hose in the event of a leakage, which he should stop with a hose cramp. In rolling up the hose, which should be previously cleaned from mud, the same order should be observed as in rolling out, each man coiling up his length, and stowing it in the Engine, the swivel nut being kept outside, as it is first required in connecting the lengths.

Any member leaving the Company's service must send in his uniform and equipments without delay.

The age for retiring from the Brigade is 45, those members who are now over that age will have to retire at 50.

It is desirable that all members of the Fire Brigade should reside within a radius of a quarter of a mile from the Works. Any members changing their present residence will be required to reside within that radius.

8

The rates of pay at all times when on duty will be as under :—

			Per Hour.	
Captain	-	-	1s.	0d.
Sergeants	-	-	0s.	10d.
Firemen	-	-	0s.	8d.

The allowance for turning out to fires other than those on the Company's property is as follows :— -

			First Hour.			Every Additional Hour.	
Superintendent	-		4s.	0d.	-	1s.	6d.
Captain	-	-	3s.	0d.	-	1s.	3d.
Firemen	-	-	2s.	0d.	-	1s.	0d.
Pumpers	-	-	1s.	0d.	-	0s.	6d.

Each member of the Brigade will be furnished with a printed copy of these Rules and Regulations, which they are enjoined carefully to preserve, and read over at least once a week.

BY ORDER.

APPENDIX IV

AN AGITATOR FROM WOLVERTON

The small collection of material still preserved at Wolverton and not yet transferred to the archives of the British Transport Commission contains an interesting sequence of three letters, written in 1901. They form part of a correspondence between Mr J. N. Emmett, Superintendent of the London and North Western's Wagon Department at Earlestown, Lancashire, and Mr C. A. Park, who was in charge at Wolverton, and illustrate the problems faced by railway management when a decision had to be taken on a matter not covered by the ordinary rules and traditional discipline.

On December 4, 1901, Mr Emmet wrote to Mr Park as follows:

Dear Sir,

I am asked to sanction shop meetings being held at Earlestown, prior to memorialising the Directors for (a) three days leave and pay for same once a year, and (b) an annual free pass for every workman and his wife. It appears that one of your workpeople came over here on Saturday last, and met, by appointment, several of the men out of the Works, who had been got together at the request of your man, who stated that you had already consented to shop meetings being held at Wolverton for the purpose as above. He further said you had also promised to present such a memorial to the Directors if submitted to you.

Having in mind the recent negative decision of the Directors to a very similar application on the part of my men at the Willesden Repairing Shop, I am anxious to know if there is any truth whatever in the statement made by one of your workpeople on Saturday last. Your early reply will oblige.

Mr Park replied the following day:

Dear Sir,

Referring to your letter of the 4th instant. I have not consented to the shop meetings being held in the Works here, and so far as I know none have been held. I may say for your information that some time ago a memorial similar to the one you mention was presented by my men, and I submitted it to the General Manager, who could not see his way to entertain it, and the workmen were duly informed of the decision through my Works Manager. Can you give me the name of the workman from here who spoke to your people about the matter on Saturday last.

Mr Emmett carried out further research and reported back on 9 December.

Dear Sir,

Accept my thanks for your favour of the 5th instant. I have made further enquiries into the subject matter of my letter of the 4th and now learn that a Committee was formed at Wolverton, some twelve months ago, for the purpose of agitating for additional privileges being granted to the men. This Committee would, I presume be the one instrumental in bringing to your notice the memorial to which you refer. Failing to accomplish their object in this manner, it appears that the Executive Committee is now asking my men, and afterwards the men in the Locomotive Department, Crewe, to co-operate with yours so that by combined action one huge memorial may be presented to the Directors as from the men in the Locomotive, Carriage and Wagon Departments, and it is with this object in view that your man, Snowdon, a Finisher I believe, came here to solicit the sympathy and co-operation of my workmen.

The campaign for paid holidays was a long one and, at Wolverton as elsewhere, regular holidays were allowed many years before the principle of paying for them was accepted. The correspondence reproduced here should be read in conjunction with Mr Healey's memories, quoted above on pp. 48-49.

NOTES

1. The Perishability of Rule Books

1. *The First Industrial Nation*, p. 151.
2. Ibid., p. 153.
3. 'Factory Discipline in the Industrial Revolution', in *Economic History Review*, 1963, No. 2, and, subsequently, in *The Genesis of Modern Management*, 1965, which has a full bibliography. Valuable information is also contained in N. McKendrick's article, 'Josiah Wedgwood and Factory Discipline', in the *Historical Journal*, 1961, No. 1.
4. 'Factory Discipline in the Industrial Revolution', p. 254. 'Belper Round Mill,' Professor Pollard notes, 'was built like a Benthamite Panoplicon: an overseer at the centre had a clear view of what went on in all the eight segments.' (p. 258).
5. Ibid., p. 258.
6. Ibid., p. 201.
7. Ibid., pp. 261-2.
8. 'A note on the Supply of Staff for the Early Railways', in *Transport History*, Vol. 1, No. 1, March 1968.
9. 'The Railway Towns of Southern England', in *Transport History*, Vol. 2, No. 2, July 1969.
10. Despite the large number of railway works which existed by the end of the nineteenth century. The Great Western alone had ten. No works rule books are included in George Ottley's monumental work, *A Bibliography of British Railway History* (1965). Mr Ottley notes: 'Every Company had its rules and regulations for employees . . . and I have thought it sufficient for our purpose to include a selection from those which have come to hand in the course of compiling.' (p. 16). The examples chosen by Mr Ottley cover only the operating side.

2. The Pioneering Rules

1. *First Report* paragraphs 4540-3.
2. Entrance or gratitude money, payable when a man took up a new job.
3. Notices of this kind were sadly frequent at Shildon. They continued throughout the fifties and sixties. An announcement of 15 December 1866 reads: 'In consequence of the depression in trades it is proposed to make a General Reduction in wages at these works to 'take effect from 14 January 1867. At the same time it is proposed to reduce the Time worked by extending the time allowed for dinner from 12.50 p.m. to 1 o'clock p.m.'
   1 SAD 4/134
   These reductions in wages could, like short-time working, be applied to particular individuals. In 1841, for instance, this record occurs:

'George Scott   Present Wages 5s. 6d.—reduce 6d. per day
Jas. Robinson   2s. 6d.—to have three days of work'
The same entry reports that an engineman and fireman were 'turned
off refractory'. They had no redress.

4. 1847 was a particularly miserable year for the men. On 28 December
they were put on three-quarter time.

5. On the other hand, the Railway Birthday on 27 September was
always celebrated, no matter what the state of trade might be, by
allowing the men to go home at 4 o'clock with no loss of wages.

6. SAD 15/2.

7. The railways were in exactly the same position as any other employer.
There was, for instance, a sellers' market for skilled glass-makers in the
1840's, following the repeal of Excise Duty on glass. This produced
much labour-trouble, with frequent bribing away and movement from
one employer to another. In 1845 Pilkington's workers were persuaded
to sign new six-year contracts—they had asked for the customary seven—
and they each received a premium of £15 on signature. In return, they
agreed to a clause giving the masters power to suspend for up to a
week at a time for disobedience or non-attendance without cause. On
this see T. C. Barker, *Pilkington Brothers and the Glass Industry*, pp.
106–7.

8. BTHR WEL 1/52.

9. Subsequent editions of the rules of the railway provident and pension
societies contained very similar provisions. The L.M.S. Rules, as revised in 1924, said: 'Should any member be disabled for work in
consequence of immoral conduct, intemperance, or by injury through
quarrelling or fighting, or impair his mental faculties by drinking, or
meet with an accident while under the influence of intoxicating liquors,
in such case he shall not have any claim upon the Society's funds.'

3. The Rule Books and the Factory Acts

1. BTHR MID 4/159/11.

2. With the navvies, discipline was largely a matter of personality. The
great contractor, Thomas Brassey, was a man of very strong personality. From his navvies, 'he received absolute devotion and loyalty'. He
paid more than the accepted rates, disliked Unions and 'if he under-
took a difficult and unprofitable contract he never let his men lose'.
And when times were hard and contracts were few, he phased his
work, often to his own disadvantage, so that they should stay
employed and cushioned. (Charles Walker: *Thomas Brassey, Railway
Builder* p. 165.) In his and other cases paternalism was a success.
Brunel had a similar gift. He 'found his navvies "very manageable",
but he had a talent for getting on with his men . . . the men were not
all devoid of the Victorian values. They could be grateful to a
competent master.' (Terry Coleman: *The Railway Navvies*, p. 29).

4. Controlling the workers at Swindon

1. The locomotive works at Swindon were finished in 1813. For many years they were used only for repairs and overhauls. The first engine was built there in 1846. In the next two years large sums were spent on new shops and new machinery. By 1848, 1800 men were employed at Swindon Works. In 1849 the number was reduced to 600, as the result of a slump in railway business. Further expansion took place in 1853–4. When he laid the foundation stone of the new shops, Daniel Gooch took the opportunity to mention that during the sixteen years he had been connected with the Company no strike or other symptom of disaffection between the workmen and directors had occurred.

2. This is the earliest Swindon rule-book I have been able to discover. It is certainly a revision of an earlier document, probably of the late 1880's or 1890's. Mr C. W. Love, who very kindly lent it to me, signed this section at the end:

   'I, the undersigned, having been appointed as Boy in the service of the Great Western Railway Company, do hereby bind myself to observe and obey the foregoing rules and regulations; and hereby declare that I have carefully read them (or have had them read to me) and that I clearly understand them and have received a copy of the same.'

   Mr Love told me that until the 1920's all apprentices at the Works started as office-boys. After a few months running errands around the Works in this way, they had absorbed a good deal of the atmosphere and organisation of the place and were considered fit to begin the serious business of their apprenticeship.

3. An exception to this rule was made for the men working in the Rolling Mills and Foundry, at least as early as 1905. They were accustomed to drink a gallon of beer a day and sent a boy out for it.

4. At Swindon, during the first quarter of the present century, the main form of trading within the Works was money-lending. Money was lent by these financial specialists to their fellow-workmen in units of a shilling, on which the interest was a half-penny a week.

5. I have quoted here from the Readers Library edition of 1920.

6. One should perhaps mention that managerial posts in the railway workshops were highly desirable and much sought after. They were well paid and provided considerable opportunity for the exercise of power.

   In 1870, Mr W. Dean, who was in charge of No. 2 Works at Swindon, received a salary of £600 a year, out of which he paid 19s. 3d. a month income tax and £1 3s. 1d. a month towards his superannuation.

   Other managers at Swindon had £450 and £250 a year, excellent salaries in 1870. They were privileged people in the town.

   Details of Swindon salaries at this date are to be found in BTHR GW/15/194.

5. Wolverton and Stratford

1. Ms. autobiography, written in 1954. In a conversation with the present author, Mr Healey emphasised that entrance was easier for the sons of men employed in the Works. 'If you worked in the Works, you could get your son in and get him a trade.' His own son started when he left school, as an apprentice body-builder.
2. Ibid.
3. Ibid.
4. Ibid. On the campaign for holidays, see the correspondence in Appendix IV.
5. Mr Healey remembers having such a rule book, 'a little red book', but says he had to hand it back when he left the railway service. It seems very likely that the Company held regular bonfires of these returned rule books.
6. Handwritten, like nearly all the notices of the pre-1914 period, both at Wolverton and elsewhere.
7. See below, *Great Eastern Rules*, Rule IX.
8. RB 1 339.

6. Crewe and Derby

1. It contains no indication of the author or the publisher.
2. On this see W. H. Chaloner, 'Francis William Webb', in *Transport History*, Vol. 1, No. 2, July 1968.
3. The railway managements were not alone in their firm attitude towards smoking. It has always been a major industrial hazard, especially in the days of oil-soaked wooden floors, when a match could all too easily send the workshop or factory up in flames. There was, however, another good reason for banning it in an engineering shop. Smoking meant stopping work for a while, in order to wipe some of the grease off one's hands, take a pipe out of one's pocket, cut up twist, fill the pipe, strike six matches, and get it going. All this caused a great waste of time. Smoking in 1910 did not mean what smoking means today. As factory-made cigarettes became more common, the no-smoking rule was gradually relaxed, at least in some parts of the Works.
4. I am indebted to Mr R. A. Riddles for these details.
5. Communication from Mr Leslie Cooper.
6. In the opinion of Mr R. A. Riddles. Conversation with the author, August 1969. Riddles joined the L.N.W.R. in 1909 as a premium apprentice at Crewe Works. During the 1920's he introduced a progressive system for locomotive repairs which considerably reduced time and cost. He was later in charge of the large-scale reorganisation of Crewe Works. In 1928 he went to Derby as Assistant Locomotive Works Superintendent, and in 1931 returned to Crewe as Assistant Locomotive Works Superintendent. In 1931 he became Locomotive Assistant to Sir William Stanier, the Chief Mechanical Engineer, and in 1935 Principal Assistant.

7. This extra security was very real. During 1925–7, Crewe got rid of 1,000 men in a few months. The foremen picked the men they wanted to keep, and, generally speaking, the best men stayed. There was no rule of last-in, first-out.
8. Conversation with the author, August 1969.
9. Foremen walked around constantly and a man had to have a very good reason for being outside his own working area. After 1918 a policeman was appointed to challenge people.
10. Conversation with the author, June 1969.
11. I should like to express my gratitude to Mr Pearce for the invaluable conversation I had with him during the summer of 1969.
12. Not all apprentices were engaged in this way. Time-keeping at Derby was carried out by means of brass checks, controlled by the Time Office. These checks were returned to the men at their place of work twice a day, in the late morning and late afternoon, by 14–15 year old boys employed for the purpose. When these check-boys grew older, they were offered the chance of choosing a trade and most of them did so.
13. One interesting reflection of the difference between Swindon and Crewe, on the one hand, and Derby on the other was that, right up to the outbreak of war in 1914, most men at the Railway Works at Derby contributed to a medical fund of their own choosing, not to the Company's. The Company had a Friendly Society, but the men did not take full advantage of it.
14. Suspension became less and less frequent after the First World War and by the mid-twenties it had virtually ceased.

7. The old discipline weakens

1. Preserved in BTHR BR RB1/406. It was reprinted without change in 1945.

8. The Rules become popularised

1. BR 7013/8. This is the sub-title. In much larger letters across the top of the cover is the eye-catching, sex-loaded, main title, *The Facts of Life*.